Breed Standard

Co
Wh
live
ran
rec
che

wards
tip,
ering,
th

C
D
d
f
f
r

tail;
t
able.

I
F
a
developed pads.

D1420729

DISTRIBUTED BY: **INTERPET** PUBLISHING

Vincent Lane, Dorking, Surrey RH4 3YX England

Labrador Retriever

by Bernard Duke

Table of Contents

ISBN 13: 978-0-966859-23-2

Origins of the Labrador Retriever

What introduction does the world's most popular dog require? Everyone has seen a Labrador romping happily with his family. Regarded as the ideal family dog for generations, the Labrador is by definition biddable and adaptable to practically any lifestyle.

It's common today to hear the breed simply referred to as the Labrador, however, this is by and large incorrect. The Labrador is a retriever. The Labrador Retriever, a prominent member of the Gundog Group, is a hunting dog by trade. The pet Labrador Retriever comes from a genealogy of hard-working hunters who could spend tireless hours on upland game birds on rigorous terrain.

While your pet Labrador Retriever may only fetch your slippers and the Sunday paper, it is helpful to understand that his grandfathers pursued pheasant, duck and other wild fowl.

Well, that's the 'retriever' part of his name: what's the meaning of the 'Labrador' part? To truly understand the breed's origins, we must look not to Labrador, but to the island off its southern shores

Labrador Retrievers are bred in three colours: black, liver/ chocolate or yellow.

Labrador Retriever puppy. Originally this breed was called the Lesser Newfoundland Dog.

called Newfoundland. The rich history of this island, originally inhabited by the Dorset Eskimos, dates back to the 1400s; however it wasn't until the 1600s that the island became the home of wayward fishermen. These fishermen, it is believed, swam to the island after abandoning ships that were passing by the island. As fishermen tend to be 'free spirits' (like many today!), the island went without laws or establishments of any kind for the next two centuries, despite the inhabitation of these men.

The first dogs on the island of Newfoundland are traced to these fishermen, as there is no evidence of the Eskimos' having dogs on the island, and no dogs existed on Newfoundland when the fishermen landed there. As the Labrador Retriever was once called the Lesser Newfoundland Dog, it has often been presumed that the breed is related to the Newfoundland breed. This breed, well known to dog lovers today, is a much larger, more abundantly coated, heavy-boned dog, showing much influence of its mastiff origins. Still, both the Newfoundland and the Labrador Retriever share the unique physical characteristic of webbed feet.

The terrain and weather conditions of Newfoundland are rugged, requiring a dog of sure-footedness, stamina, and 'buoyancy.' The size of the Labrador Retriever mattered tremendously, and a small dog was necessary to fit into the fishermen's dory. The dogs' webbed feet speak well for the Labrador's ability to swim, even in the icy, rough waters of the North Atlantic. Among the other characteristics of our modern Labradors that 'make sense' for a dog surviving on Newfoundland's brutal shores is the thick and waterproof coat required. Another important feature of the breed is its broad chest, necessary for 'surfing' against the strong waves and current of the unrelenting North Atlantic. Since the island was bountiful in game, the fishermen were able to use their dogs to

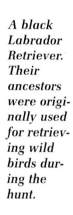

A black Labrador Retriever. Their ancestors were originally used for retrieving wild birds during the hunt.

While Labrador Retrievers have been useful for many tasks through their noble history, they have always been treasured as trustworthy family pets.

deemed them the dogs of choice. The retrievers soon replaced the pointers and setters that had stood beside these sportsmen. Although the Labrador Retriever that we know today comes in three acceptable colours, black, yellow and chocolate, the dogs on New-foundland were principally black. These small black dogs were sometimes referred to as St. John's Water Dogs, and were called 'the best of any kind of dog for shoot-ing...by far.'

A frustrating fact to breed enthusiasts today is that the resi-dents of Newfoundland kept no records of the dogs on which they relied upon so heavily. Survival on this barren island was such an all-encompassing pursuit that there was little time for such record-keeping.

supplement their food supply from the land as well as the sea. The Newfoundlanders were importing quality retriever stock from England, though there was considerable variation in type. The division of the retriever breeds came much later, and at this time (circa 1780–1810) any retriever, longhaired, curlycoated, shortcoated, wavycoated, was bred to produce other retrievers of excellent working ability.

Labradors weren't the only dogs on the island at this point, as settlers brought other types; how-ever, as the reputation of the Labrador grew, these dogs were often replaced with Labradors. Since the Labrador's disposition and adaptability were so highly respected, hunters and sportsmen

THE LABRADOR COMES TO BRITAIN

The Second and Third Earls of Malmsbury are credited for

DID YOU KNOW?

The behaviour and personality of your Labrador Retriever will reflect your care and training more than any breed characteristics or indications. Remem-ber that these dogs require a purpose-ful existence and plan your relation-ship around activities that serve this most basic and important need. All the good potential of the breed will necessarily follow.

exporting these famous St. John's Dogs from Newfoundland to Great Britain. The dogs at this point in time (around 1825) were sometimes called Little Newfoundlers. The Third Earl, the pioneer breeder of these dogs, is credited for changing the name to Labrador Retriever. These gentry and others like them kept the Labradors pure, breeding them only to dogs imported from Newfoundland, as they were exceptional for their swimming, retrieving and fighting abilities. It is also said that any of the puppies from these St. John's Dogs that were crossed to other dogs usually maintained the strong appearance of the Labrador—black, short fur, a non-curling tail and the webbed feet.

As early as the 1870s the 'breed' was described as symmetrical and elegant, and the temperament was praised and considered a requirement for the utility of the Labrador. It's no doubt that the early breeders' commitment to a sound disposition in the Labrador contributed to the breed's enormous popularity as a family dog around the world.

In 1903 the Labrador Retriever was recognised by The Kennel Club. The following year the breed was listed separately as a member of the Gundog Group. The retrievers at this point were still not divided by 'breed' as we know them today. It was not until the year 1904, when the Labrador Retriever was separately listed,

The Third Earl of Malmsbury established the name Labrador Retriever for the breed. The Labs shown are typical English-bred dogs.

that The Kennel Club began to differentiate between 'breeds.' There is confusion in the records from these early days because some dogs were called 'golden' and oth-

The Lab was recognised by The Kennel Club in 1903.

ers 'Labrador', though there is no indication about coat length. Thus, the 'golden retrievers' may have indeed been yellow Labrador Retrievers. This was the early days of purebred dog enthusiasm. It must be stated today that many people in the general public do not know the difference between a yellow Labrador and the Golden Retriever (despite the long, wavy, luxurious coat of the latter). As a rule, we never call a yellow Labrador a 'golden' Labrador.

The Kennel Club's stud books contain references to liver-coloured wavycoated retrievers: these dogs in actuality trace back to the chocolate Labrador Retrievers of the famous Buccleuch Kennels, the breeders responsible for six of the seven of the first retrievers entered in the stud book. Buccleuch Kennels produced the famous field trial champion by the name of Peter of Faskally, who is known to be behind many of the top Labradors from the early days as well as many of the top field

In 1904 the Labrador Retriever was classified as a member of the Gundog Group by The Kennel Club.

Labrador Retrievers are famous for their stamina and physical abilities, like running, swimming and jumping.

dogs in England and the U.S. Many of the breed books still in print depict these famous dual champions.

The best yellow Labrador Retrievers are traced back to a dog by the name of Ben of Hyde, who was whelped in 1899. He was bred to many excellent black bitches, and his genes are buttoned on the top yellow Lab kennels in all of England. While the blacks have always predominated the other two colours, the period after World War Two marked an increase in the yellow Labs' popularity.

Lorna, Countess Howe, in cahoots with Lord Knutsford, founded the Labrador Club in 1916 and held the first field trial in 1920. Lord Knutsford authored the first Labrador Retriever standard in 1923. The standard is a written description of the ideal specimen of the breed. Knutsford's standard has changed very little to the present day. Countess Howe, considered the greatest of Labrador breeders, produced a number of dual

Black Labs are more numerous than yellow or chocolate.

champions—that is, dogs titled as a bench (show) champion and a field trial champion. Not the least of Countess Howe's great Labradors was the first dual champion of the breed, Dual Champion Banchory Bolo, the son of her very first

Labrador, Scandal. It was Bolo with whom Countess Howe was most enamoured, the dog who made her truly head over hocks for the Labrador Retriever breed.

The Royal Family has long been associated with the Labrador. King George VI and Queen Eliza-

King George VI and Queen Elizabeth promoted Labrador Retrievers through their royal kennels.

beth promoted Labradors at shows through their kennel known as Wolverton (more recently changed to Sandringham). The King entered dogs in Crufts in the 1920s and '30s. The Queen actually entered field trials with her dogs—just to illustrate the kinds of people attracted to field trials in England! George was the Patron of the Labrador Club, and was replaced by Elizabeth as Patroness

after his death. Today in England, field trials are still supported by the Royal Family, and the annual championship is held at the Queen's shooting estate, Sandringham, in East Anglia. She is often in attendance at the British Retriever Championship in December.

The British shooting dogs, or working gun dogs, are athletic in type and appearance. In order for a dog to excel in a field trial, it must possess discipline, control and responsiveness. Of course it is much more difficult for a dog to achieve a field trial championship in Britain than it would be in the U.S., where field trials are mere and remote imitations of hunting. In the U.K., where the shooting sport originated, a field trial is an actual hunting episode, including wild birds and whatever else Mother Nature supplies. What makes hunting exciting is the surprise, and that element is essential to a field trial as well. The American field-trial counterparts revel in the robot-like performances of their atypical Labradors. The English field dogs look more like Labradors, by and large; not because the sportsmen care more about type than the Americans, but because they do not rely on such regimented trials. The natural abilities of the dogs, not hindered by the collar conditioning and training common to Americans, are the main focus of

British sportsmen. Secondly, the stable temperament of the English field dogs, compared to the more high-strung American field dogs, hints at the superiority of the British system, where nature, temperament and talent combine to make the ideal Labrador hunting companion.

Of course the landscape of Long Island paints the perfect setting for a working Labrador Retriever, with the abundance of waterfowl, its rolling oceanfront and its extreme temperatures. To say that the Labrador Retriever caught on in America immediately would not be true. Although the breed was first

Lady Howe sent the first Labrador Retrievers to the U.S.A. immediately after World War I and the first dog was registered with the AKC in 1917.

THE FIRST LABRADORS ON AMERICAN SHORES

America extends its gratitude to Lorna, Countess Howe for exporting the first Labradors 'back' to North American shores. Lest we forget, the Labrador began on Canadian shores! Sportsmen in Long Island, New York, were gifted by Lady Howe with the first Labradors to be seen in the U.S. This occurred shortly after the First World War.

registered with the American Kennel Club in 1917, ten years later there were scarcely two dozen retrievers (of all types!) in the U.S. The first Labrador registered was a bitch of Scottish origin by the name of Brocklehirst Floss (AKC #223339). The breed was officially recognised in 1932. The average American, middle class, so to speak, was not the original keeper of the Labrador, as they are today. Instead the upper class wealthy families were attracted to shooting sports, popular in Scotland in the 1920s. These families brought gamekeepers from Scotland onto their estates and imported Labradors from the finest

The Lab was used in the U.S.A. to retrieve birds for hunters.

English kennels, virtually converting their estates into shooting preserves, chockfull of ducks and pheasants. It's important to note that these Labradors were imported for one purpose only: not to become beloved family pets or show dogs, but 'to retrieve upland game and waterfowl.' These same gentlefolk are responsible for the rise of field trials in America and thus the birth of The Labrador Retriever Club in 1931 in New York State. Franklin B. Lord, one of the club's founding members, held the club's first field trial in December 1931. A total of 27 dogs competed under two judges on a 8000-acre estate. The club's first dog show occurred some 18 months later in 1933, attracting 33 dogs. The winner of the first show was owned by Mr. Lord, a dog by the name of Boli of Blake, bred by Countess Howe. Boli also became the first bench champion of the breed.

This national parent club, affiliated with the AKC, is the most controversial club in the U.S. Like the Westminster Kennel Club, the Labrador Club, Inc. is an exclusive 'men's club', not available for membership by the average dog owner, and still dedicated to the upper class sportsmen. It does, nevertheless, defend the standard of the breed and sets the trend for the 'correct' Labrador in the U.S. The dissension in the Labrador Retriever breed in America is deep-rooted, and there is much variation in breed type as an unfortunate result. It is common

DID YOU KNOW?

Bred to be a sporting dog, the Labrador must be well balanced and strongly built in order to perform his intended function. Breed standards differ from country to country; for example, the American Kennel Club standard's height range is two inches higher than that of the Kennel Club's. Problems lie not in small variation, but in gross exaggeration. The breed's overwhelming popularity and constant demand for puppies have made the Labrador vulnerable to irresponsible breeders who seem to think that bigger is better. Beware of purchasing a pup from oversized parents, as oversize leads to physical defects. Even though a Labrador does not reach full size until about two-and-a-half years of age, balance and good proportion are still evident in the young Lab and are key characteristics upon which you should base your choice.

The controversial Labrador Retriever Club, Inc. is exclusively a men's club dedicated to upper-class sportsmen.

for judges to ignore the breed standard and award 'Best of Breed' to a dog that has gross faults, according to the standard, and probably a disqualification. The height disqualification in the revised AKC standard renders most show dogs too short to enter the ring. It is almost religiously ignored. The Labrador Retriever Club, Inc. seeks to breed and promote working-type dogs, tall enough to do the work, and not nearly as heavyset and 'pig-like' as most dogs that win in the show ring. The show ring enthusiasts claim that their dogs are not as high-strung as the hunting strains, though there is no doubt that the show dogs are not suited to last a whole day in the field retrieving upland game and waterfowl.

Despite this controversy, the Labrador Retriever, in all colours, shapes and sizes, reigns as America's number-one dog. It outregisters every other breed annually and has been on the top of the list for a decade! As a family pet, it is Americans' dog of choice. Whether or not the 100,000 plus Labradors registered every year with the AKC can hunt, swim, retrieve, or endure a day in the field seems immaterial to the millions of lovers of the pet Labrador. Its temperament and reliability, two qualities sought out by the early breeders, make it a flawless companion for dog folk of all ages.

The Labrador Retriever Club, Inc. promotes working-type dogs, which are not at all like the show dog types.

Why the Labrador Retriever?

The answer to the question, 'Why the Labrador Retriever?' too often seems to be 'Why not!' Since there are literally millions of happy Labrador lovers around the world, why shouldn't everyone love a Lab? Given the good looks, trainability, loyalty, intelligence, etc., etc., why isn't this a dog for everyone on the planet who loves dogs?! Let's begin by listing the kinds of people who should not consider the ubiquitous Labrador for their lives. Then we will examine the Labrador Retriever's character and the kinds of people who are ideal to own this talented fellow.

OWNERS BEWARE

POTENTIAL OWNERS WHO ARE LOOKING FOR A LAP DOG

The Lab is no lap dog. Sure he'll want to lap and kiss you constantly, but he's too big to sit on your lap whilst you're reading or spending time in front of the television. Labradors like to be close to you, that's for sure; but sixty pounds of true love is too much for anyone's lap!

POTENTIAL OWNERS WHO DO NOT LIKE EXERCISE

Labradors love to romp and play, preferably with their trusted owners close by. Since the breed is designed to be chasing birds in the swamp or swimming toward a fallen duck, it most definitely has 'energy to spare.' Since most Labrador owners do not have the time or inclination to take their dogs out on a weekend duck hunt, Labradors will need outlets for their abundant energy.

DID YOU KNOW?

The Labrador Retriever has been used in more areas of service to humankind than any other breed. Here are ten important areas that the breed has served:

1. Companions for all.
2. Hunting and retrieving for sportsmen.
3. Guides for the blind.
4. Hearing dogs for the deaf.
5. Arson and bomb detection.
6. Drug and substance detection.
7. Watch dogs for businesses and residences.
8. Search and rescue/avalanche and earthquake work.
9. Therapy dogs for hospitals.
10. Cancer detection.

A yellow Lab at home indoors. Labs like to be indoors with their loved ones.

POTENTIAL OWNERS WHO DO NOT HAVE A FENCED GARDEN OR ESTATE
The Labrador needs a sizeable piece of property on which to exercise, and a fence is imperative. As a gun dog, the Labrador does not have a strong sense of territory, and he will not guard his property the way a Rottweiler or Dobermann will. This is not to say that he is not protective—he is most protective of his family and home. However, more than likely, he will tear off in pursuit of a flapping pigeon or some other twittery passer-by.

POTENTIAL OWNERS WHO ARE SEEKING AN 'ORNAMENTAL' OR OUTDOOR DOG
The Labrador Retriever, for all his natural good looks and charm, does not fancy an owner that doesn't want to get up close to him and spend time with him indoors and out. Like most of the gun dogs, the Labrador likes to be near his family inside the home. Whilst it is true that the Labrador's ancestors were 'kennel dogs', today's Labrador is strongly inclined to be indoors with his master and loved ones. To keep a Labrador outdoors exclusively will be torture to the poor dog, and such owners should consider a different breed or no dog at all. While the breed is renowned for its adaptability with any lifestyle, the breed is best when kept indoors. A happy

Even though Labradors like the indoors, they do require exercise and some outdoor freedom.

Labrador is the true Labrador, and close to you is where your Labrador will want to be.

POTENTIAL OWNERS WHO ARE FUSSY ABOUT THEIR HOMES
The Labrador sheds. Even though the breed has a short, dense coat, he does not moult any less than

Even though Labs have short coats, they still shed.

any other dog. Furthermore, the Labrador is not, as a rule, a genteel or easygoing animal—he's a doggy dog, and he likes to play inside and out. Owners will have to enforce the house rules immediately with the puppy, or else he may think he can roughhouse in the house and out. Labradors can

> **DID YOU KNOW?**
> A dog with webbed feet must love to swim! Prized for their water retrieving abilities, Labradors naturally take to water and there's not many a Lab who will turn down the opportunity to get his paws wet. Pet Lab owners often enjoy runs and games of fetch on the beach with their dogs.

be raucous, rambunctious and rowdy—that's three 'R's' potential owners may have to live with.

ARE YOU A LABRADOR PERSON?
If you have breezed through the first part of this chapter, think-

ing that you are a good candidate for a Labrador, then let's explore the breed character further to help better understand what kind of a dog the Labrador Retriever really is.

For all the talents of Labrador Retrievers, always the top competitors in the nation's field trials and obedience trials, the breed is still only 'canine.' That is to say, the Labrador is not a 'superdog.' Mary Feazell, an American Labrador fancier and trainer, contends that the 95 percent of what a Labrador can grow up to be depends upon the owner; only 5 percent depends on the dog itself. Such a huge responsibility for the owner of this fabulously talented dog. There is little that a Labrador cannot learn. Some Labradors recognise hundreds of words and

These Labrador puppies from the same litter are remarkably similar in looks.

It has been said that 95 percent of what a Labrador can be depends upon the owner.

can execute dozens of commands. Feazell says, 'Being realistic, Labs swim well, but they can't walk on water.'

A Labrador Retriever requires a dedicated owner, whether the pursuit is basic obedience (such as sit, stay, come, the commands necessary for a well-trained home companion) or more lofty pursuits like obedience trials, field trials, agility trials, working trials, etc. Many Labrador Retrievers are so intelligent and have such a strong desire to please that they become 'self-trained.' Labradors are excellent problem-solvers and quickly decide what pleases their masters and what does not! Such self-learned abilities include coming when called, staying where he's put, not bolt-ing through the front door every time it is opened, not jumping up on visitors, permitting people to pet and touch him, not messing in the house, etc. Do not misunderstand. Labradors are smart, but you must be there to show the dog right from wrong. This is no different than instructing a child. Parents must be present for their children if they are to mature properly. Absent parents do not discipline, teach or help their children. Labradors must receive enough training to make them capable of self-control, amenable to obeying commands, and minding their owner's wishes.

The owner controls what kind of dog his Labrador becomes. The owner provides the dog with

Labrador puppies require dedicated owners. Your Labrador puppy will enjoy a romp on the beach with you.

Any properly trained Lab can learn to stand and pose like a champion.

training and guidance, encouragement, outlets for his energy and industry. The Labrador who doesn't have proper 'parental guidance' can develop behavioural problems, including destructive habits, aggression, and fear-biting, to name a few. The owner moulds his Labrador into the dog whom he wants to live with. Investing time, money and love into a dog can pay off a thousandfold; skimping on the time and education a dog as active and bright as a Labrador requires can be an owner's worst mistake. Do not rush into the ownership of a Labrador. This is a breed that deserves a top-quality owner, and if you're not sure about the acquisition, delay your decision. Read more about the breed, talk to breeders, owners and trainers, attend a dog show and meet people who commit their lives to the dogs, and then you'll be better prepared to take the dive into dog ownership.

For those of you who are certain that a Labrador Retriever is the dog that you want to share your life with, this wonderful dog can become your world. Whether it's a pet companion dog, show dog, field and working dog you require, the Labrador Retriever can become all you want in a faithful canine friend.

27

Breed Standard for the Labrador Retriever

A Lab must have an excellent nose and soft mouth.

THE KENNEL CLUB STANDARD FOR THE LABRADOR RETRIEVER
General Appearance: Strongly built, short-coupled, very active; broad in skull; broad and deep through chest and ribs; broad and strong over loins and hindquarters.

Characteristics: Good-tempered, very agile. Excellent nose, soft mouth; keen love of water. Adaptable, devoted companion.

A champion-quality black Labrador Retriever, strongly built.

Labs must be intelligent, keen and biddable, besides having beautiful, strong bodies.

Temperament: Intelligent, keen and biddable, with a strong will to please. Kindly nature, with no trace of aggression or undue shyness.

Head and Skull: Skull broad with defined stop; clean-cut without fleshy cheeks. Jaws of medium length, powerful not snipy. Nose wide, nostrils well developed.

Eyes: Medium size, expressing intelligence and good temper; brown or hazel.

Ears: Not large or heavy, hanging close to head and set rather far back.

A Lab's eyes must be of medium size and express intelligence and friendliness.

29

Mouth: Jaws and teeth strong with a perfect, regular and complete scissors bite, i.e., upper teeth closely overlapping lower teeth and set square to the jaws.

Neck: Clean, strong, powerful, set into well placed shoulders.

Forequarters: Shoulders long and sloping. Forelegs well boned and straight from elbow to ground when viewed from either front or side.

Body: Chest of good width and depth, with well sprung barrel ribs. Level topline. Loins wide, short-coupled and strong.

Hindquarters: Well developed, not sloping to tail; well turned stifle. Hocks well let down, cowhocks highly undesirable.

Feet: Round, compact; well arched toes and well developed pads.

Tail: Distinctive feature, very thick towards base, gradually tapering towards tip, medium length, free from feathering, but clothed thickly all round with short, thick, dense coat, thus giving 'rounded' appearance described as 'Otter' tail. May be carried gaily but should not curl over back.

Labs must be black, yellow or liver/chocolate like this one.

Photo by Carol Ann Johnson.

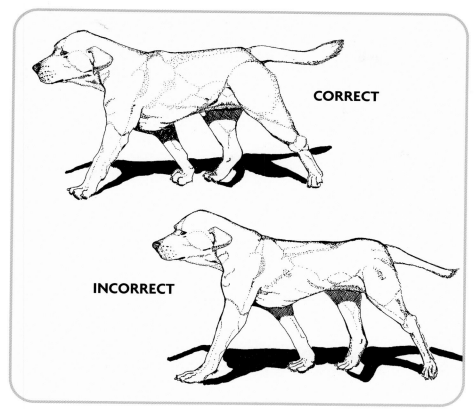

CORRECT

INCORRECT

A very distinctive feature of the Lab is its tail. The body should be solid, with the chest of good width and depth, and with well-sprung barrel ribs. The topline should be level.

Gait/Movement: Free, covering adequate ground; straight and true in front and rear.

Coat: Distinctive feature, short dense without wave or feathering, giving fairly hard feel to the touch; weather-resistant undercoat.

Colour: Wholly black, yellow or liver/chocolate. Yellows range from light cream to red fox. Small white spot on chest permissible.

Size: Ideal height at withers: dogs: 56–57 cms (22–22.5 ins); bitches: 54–56 cms (21.5–22 ins).

Faults: Any departure from the foregoing points should be considered a fault and the seriousness with which the fault should be regarded should be in exact proportion to its degree.

Note: Male animals should have two apparently normal testicles fully descended into the scrotum.

31

	CORRECT	**INCORRECT**

EARS
Set rather far back and hanging close to the head.

BITE
Teeth should meet in a perfect, regular and complete scissor bite; lower jaw should not be undershot.

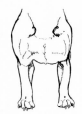

FOREQUARTERS
Forelegs should be well-boned and straight from elbow to ground; not bowing out at the shoulder.

FEET
Round, compact, with well-arched toes; not pigeon toed or splay footed.

TAIL
The distinctive 'Otter' tail should appear rounded; carried gaily but never curling over back.

HINDQUARTERS
Well developed, not sloping to tail; cowhocks are highly undesirable.

Your Labrador Retriever Puppy

OWNER CONSIDERATIONS

A purebred dog as versatile and talented as the Labrador Retriever attracts many admirers. Whether you are seeking a puppy simply as a house companion and family pet, a show dog, a field dog, or a competition dog, there are many serious factors governing your choice. You believe that you have enough time to devote to your new Labrador. Even a pet Labrador will require considerable time to train. Naturally, a field dog or obedience/agility dog will require hours of daily attention and special training. Do not take the acquisition of a Labrador Retriever lightly. This is a demanding dog who will want to share his whole life with you. The Labrador Retriever usually lives ten to fourteen years, which is a considerable portion of your human life. Do you know where you will be in a decade? You have to plan for a Labrador Retriever to be a part of that picture.

Labs need space in which to exercise outdoors. The facilities you have available should be factored into your decision when buying a dog.

Consider the exercise that a dog as active as the Labrador will require. You have a fenced garden, so there is no worry that your curious pup will not go wandering down the lane to find your neighbours and their dogs and cats and horses! If you are not committed to the welfare and whole existence of

> **DID YOU KNOW?**
> Your puppy should have a well-fed appearance but not a distended abdomen, which may indicate worms or incorrect feeding, or both. The body should be firm, with a solid feel. The skin of the abdomen should be pale pink and clean, without signs of scratching or rash. Check the hind legs to make certain that dewclaws were removed, if any were present at birth.

this energetic, purposeful animal; if, in the simplest, most basic example, you are not willing to walk your dog daily, despite the weather, do not choose a Labrador Retriever as a companion.

The safest way to buy a Lab puppy is through a reputable breeder.

Space is another important consideration. The Labrador Retriever in early puppyhood may be well accommodated in a corner of your kitchen but after only six months when the dog is likely over 60 pounds, larger space certainly will be required. You will have to train your Labrador to understand the house rules, so that you can trust him in every room of your house. Of course, puppy-proofing is vital.

Along with these factors there are the usual problems associated with puppies of any breed like the damages likely to be sustained by your floors, furniture, flowers and, not least of all, to your freedom (of movement), as in holiday or week-

end trips. This union is a serious affair and should be deeply considered but once decided, your choice of a Labrador Retriever is, perhaps, the most rewarding of all breeds. A few suggestions will help in the purchase of your dog.

ACQUIRING A PUPPY
The safest method of obtaining your puppy is to seek out a

DID YOU KNOW?

Two important documents you will get from the breeder are the pup's pedigree and registration papers. The breeder should register the litter and each pup with The Kennel Club, and it is necessary for you to have the paperwork if you plan on showing or breeding in the future.

Make sure you know the breeder's intentions on which type of registration he will obtain for the pup. There are limited registrations which may prohibit the dog from being shown or from competing in non-conformation trials such as Working or Agility if the breeder feels that the pup is not of sufficient quality to do so. There is also a type of registration that will permit the dog in non-conformation competition only.

If your dog is registered with a Kennel-Club-recognised breed club, then you can register the pup with The Kennel Club yourself. Your breeder can assist you with the specifics of the registration process.

local reputable breeder. This is suggested even if you are not looking for a show specimen or a top contender in field work. The novice breeders and pet owners who advertise at attractive prices in the local newspapers are probably kind enough toward their dogs, but perhaps do not have the expertise or facilities required to successfully raise these animals. A lack of proper feeding can cause indigestion, rickets, weak bones, poor teeth and other problems. Veterinary bills may soon distort initial

---

DID YOU KNOW?

Another important consideration to be discussed is the sex of your puppy. For a family companion, a Labrador Retriever bitch is the better choice, considering the female's inbred concern for all young creatures and her accompanying tolerance and patience. If you do not intend to spay your pet when she has matured or is well over her growing period, then extra care is required during the times of her heat.

---

savings into financial, or worse, emotional loss.

Inquire about inoculations and when the puppy was last dosed for worms. Check the ears. Ear mite infestation is very common in young puppies. Left untreated, mite infestation can damage a pup's hearing. Keep on guard for the pup's scratching or shaking its head.

Colour is a matter of personal choice, but whichever colour you prefer, your puppy should have good pigment. In black Labradors, everything is black; likewise in chocolates, the dog's nose and paws should match his colour. Yellows have black noses. The shades of yellows and chocolates can vary considerably, but avoid white markings, tan marks on chocolates, or patches of brindle (combination of brown and black hairs). While no importance is placed on colour in the breed, only the three colors—yellow, black, and chocolate—are recognised as true Labradors.

You can meet reputable breeders or get good referrals by attending a local dog show.

The colour of the Lab you acquire is strictly a matter of personal choice.

Have your newly acquired Labrador puppy examined by your local veterinary surgeon as soon as you buy it. You will want to know about possible physical defects as well as start your pup on a vaccination programme.

Note the way your choice moves. The Labrador Retriever, even in puppyhood, should show light and swift movement with no tendency to stumble or drag the hind feet. Look at the mouth to make sure that the bite is fairly even, although maturity can often correct errors present at puppyhood. If you have any doubts, ask to see the parents' mouths. This brings up an important point—do not purchase a puppy without first seeing at least one of the parents.

DID YOU KNOW?

The cost of food must also be mentioned. This is not a breed that can be maintained on table scraps and light supplement. Labrador Retrievers need a good supply of protein to develop the bone and muscle required in a working animal. Labrador Retrievers are not picky eaters but unless fed properly they can quickly succumb to skin problems.

Male dogs of this breed are equally devoted and loyal but have the drawback of being in season all year and, therefore, prone to possible wandering. This is the central reason why females are always chosen as guide dogs for the blind.

COMMITMENT OF OWNERSHIP

After considering all of these factors, you have most likely already made some very important decisions about selecting your puppy. You have chosen a Labrador Retriever, which means that you have decided which characteristics you want in a dog and what type of dog will best

Choose your puppy wisely—don't settle for second rate.

fit into your family and lifestyle. If you have selected a breeder, you have gone a step further—you have done your research and found a responsible, conscientious person who breeds quality Labrador Retrievers and who should be a reliable source of help as you and your puppy adjust to life together. If you have observed a litter in action, you have

Your home should have been prepared for the puppy's arrival. Anything potentially dangerous should be out of reach.

obtained a firsthand look at the dynamics of a puppy 'pack' and, thus, you have gotten to learn about each pup's individual personality—perhaps you have even found one that particularly appeals to you.

However, even if you have not yet found the Labrador Retriever puppy of your dreams, observing pups will help you learn to recognise certain behaviour and to determine what a pup's behaviour indicates about his temperament. You will be able to pick out which pups are the leaders, which ones are less outgoing, which ones are confident, which ones are shy, playful, friendly, aggressive, etc. Equally as important, you will learn to recognise what a healthy pup should look and act like. All

Labrador puppies are inquisitive and energetic.

of these things will help you in your search, and when you find the Labrador Retriever that was meant for you, you will know it!

Researching your breed, selecting a responsible breeder and observing as many

DID YOU KNOW?

Unfortunately, when a puppy is purchased by someone who does not take into consideration the time and attention that dog ownership requires, it is the puppy who suffers when he is either abandoned or placed in a shelter by a frustrated owner. So all of the 'homework' you do in preparation for your pup's arrival will benefit you both. The more informed you are, the more you will know what to expect and the better equipped you will be to handle the ups and downs of raising a puppy. Hopefully, everyone in the household is willing to do his part in raising and caring for the pup. The anticipation of owning a dog often brings a lot of promises from excited family members: 'I will walk him every day,' 'I will feed him,' 'I will housebreak him,' etc., but these things take time and effort, and promises can easily be forgotten once the novelty of the new pet has worn off.

pups as possible are all important steps on the way to dog ownership. It may seem like a lot of effort...and you have not even brought the pup home yet! Remember, though, you cannot be too careful when it comes to deciding on the type of dog you want and finding out about your prospective pup's background. Buying a puppy is not—or should not be—just

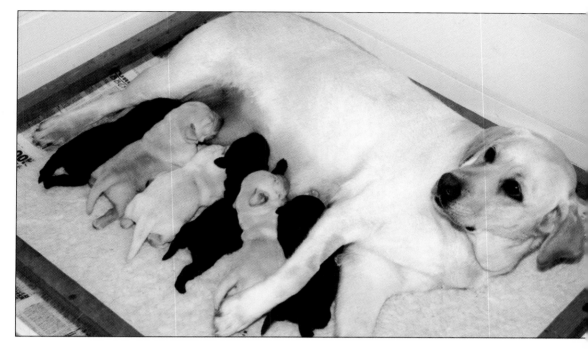

another whimsical purchase. In fact, this is one instance in which you actually *do* get to choose your own family! But, you may be thinking, buying a puppy should be fun—it should not be so serious and so much work. If you keep in mind the thought that your puppy is not a cuddly stuffed toy or decorative lawn ornament, but instead will become a real member of your family, you will realise that while buying a puppy is a pleasurable and exciting endeavour, it is not something to be taken lightly. Relax…the fun will start when the pup comes home!

Always keep in mind that a puppy is nothing more than a baby in a furry disguise…a baby who is virtually helpless in a human world and who trusts his owner for fulfilment of his basic needs for survival. That goes beyond food, water and shelter; your pup needs care, protection, guidance and love. If you are not prepared to commit to this, then you are not prepared to own a dog.

Wait a minute, you say. How hard could this be? All of my neighbours own dogs and they seem to be doing just fine. Why should I have to worry about all of this? Well, you

These Labrador puppies are too young to take home, but a breeder will often reserve the puppy you prefer until he is old enough.

should not worry about it; in fact, you will probably find that once your Labrador Retriever pup gets used to his new home, he will fall into his place in the family quite naturally. But it never hurts to emphasise the commitment of dog ownership. With some time and patience, it is really not too difficult to raise a curious and exuberant Labrador Retriever pup to be a well-adjusted and well-mannered adult dog—a dog that could be your most loyal friend.

PREPARING PUPPY'S PLACE IN YOUR HOME

Researching your breed and finding a breeder are only two aspects of the 'homework' you will have to do before bringing your Labrador Retriever puppy home. You will also have to prepare your home and family for the new addition. Much like you would prepare a nursery for a newborn baby, you will need to designate a place in your home that will be the puppy's own. How you prepare your home will depend on how much freedom the dog will be allowed: will he be confined to one room or a specific area in the house, or will he be allowed to roam as he pleases? Will he spend most of his time in the house or will he be primarily an outdoor dog? Whatever you decide, you must ensure that he has a place that he can 'call his own.'

When you bring your new puppy into your home, you are bringing him into what will become his home as well. Obviously, you did not buy a puppy so that he could take over your house, but in order for a puppy to grow into a stable, well-adjusted dog, he has to feel comfortable in his surroundings.

When you go Labrador puppy-shopping, chances are the puppy will select you before you select him.

Puppies in a basket make a nice picture, but a basket is not considered proper housing for a pup.

Remember, he is leaving the warmth and security of his mother and littermates, plus the familiarity of the only place he has ever known, so it is important to make his transition as easy as possible. By preparing a place in your home for the puppy, you are making him feel as welcome as possible in a strange new place. It should not take him long to get used to it, but the sudden shock of being transplanted is somewhat traumatic for a young pup. Imagine how a small child would feel in the same situation—that is how your puppy must be feeling. It is up to you to reassure him and to let him know, 'Little fellow, you are going to like it here!'

DID YOU KNOW?
The majority of problems that are commonly seen in young pups will disappear as your Labrador Retriever gets older. However, how you deal with problems when he is young will determine how he reacts to discipline as an adult dog. It is important to establish who is boss (hopefully it will be you!) right away when you are first bonding with your Labrador Retriever. This bond will set the tone for the rest of your life together.

A wire crate is good for use in the home as it lets the dog see what's going on around him.

WHAT YOU SHOULD BUY

CRATE

To someone unfamiliar with the use of crates in dog training, it may seem like punishment to shut a dog in a crate; this is not the case at all. Crates are not cruel—crates have many humane and highly effective uses in dog care and training. For example, crate training is a very popular and very successful housebreaking

Crates are not cruel. They are effective in care and training.

method; a crate can keep your dog safe during travel; and, perhaps most importantly, a crate provides your dog with a place of his own in your home. It serves as a 'doggie bedroom' of sorts—your Labrador

The crate is probably the most important accessory you can purchase for your Lab.

Retriever can curl up in his crate when he wants to sleep or when he just needs a break. Many dogs sleep in their crates overnight. When lined with soft blankets and his favourite toy, a crate becomes a cosy pseudo-den for your dog. Like his ancestors, he too will seek out the comfort and retreat of a den—you just happen to be providing him with something a little more luxurious than leaves and twigs lining a dirty ditch.

As far as purchasing a crate, the type that you buy is up to you. It will most likely be one of the two most popular types: wire or fibreglass. There are advantages and disadvantages to each type. For example, a wire crate is more open, allowing the air to flow through and affording the dog a view of what is going on around him. A fibreglass crate, however, is sturdier and can double as a travel crate since it provides more protection for the dog. The size of

PHOTO COURTESY OF DOSKOCIL.

for a full-grown Labrador Retriever, as their approximate weight range is between 55 and 80 pounds.

BEDDING

Veterinary bedding in the dog's crate will help the dog feel more at home. First, the bedding will take the place of the leaves, twigs, etc., that the pup would use in the wild to make a den; the pup can make his own 'burrow' in the crate. Although your pup is far removed from his den-making ancestors, the denning instinct is still a part of his genetic makeup. Second, until you bring your pup home, he has been sleeping amidst the warmth of his mother and littermates, and while a blanket

Your local pet shop can offer many types and sizes of kennels.

the crate is another thing to consider. Puppies do not stay puppies forever—in fact, sometimes it seems as if they grow right before your eyes. A Yorkie-sized crate may be fine for a very young Labrador Retriever pup, but it will not do him much good for long! Unless you have the money and the inclination to buy a new crate every time your pup has a growth spurt, it is better to get one that will accommodate your dog both as a pup and at full size. A large crate will be necessary

is not the same as a warm, breathing body, it still provides heat and something with which to snuggle. You will want to wash your pup's blankets frequently in case he has an accident in his crate, and

Blankets, old pillows or just about anything soft and snugly will be appreciated by your Lab throughout its life.

In multiple-dog households the dogs often keep themselves occupied by playing with each other.

replace or remove any blanket that becomes ragged and starts to fall apart.

Toys

Toys are a must for dogs of all ages, especially for curious playful pups. Puppies are the 'children' of the dog world, and what child does not love toys? Chew toys provide enjoyment to both dog and owner—your dog will enjoy playing with his favourite toys, while you will enjoy the fact that they distract him from your expensive shoes and leather sofa. Puppies love to chew; in fact, chewing is a physical need for pups as they are teething, and everything looks appetising! The full range of your possessions—from old dishrag to Oriental rug—are fair game in the eyes of a teething pup. Puppies are not all that discerning when it comes to finding something to

literally 'sink their teeth into'—everything tastes great!

Stuffed toys are another option; these are good to put in the dog's crate to give him some company. Be careful of these, as a pup can de-stuff one pretty quickly, and stay away from stuffed toys with small plastic eyes or parts that a pup could choke

---

DID YOU KNOW?

During crate training, you should partition off the section of the crate in which the pup stays. If he is given too big of an area, this will hinder your training efforts. Crate training is based on the fact that a dog does not like to soil his sleeping quarters, so it is ineffective to keep a pup in a crate that is so big that he can eliminate in one end and get far enough away from it to sleep. Also, you want to make the crate den-like for the pup. Blankets and a favourite toy will make the crate cosy for the small Labrador Retriever; as he grows, you may want to evict some of his 'roommates' to make more room.

It will take some coaxing at first, but be patient. Given some time to get used to it, your pup will adapt to his new home-within-a-home quite nicely.

Pet shops have a large selection of safe, durable pet toys suitable for training and entertaining your Lab.

on. Similarly, squeaky toys are quite popular. There are dogs that will come running from anywhere in the house at the first sound from their favourite squeaky friend. Again, if a pup de-stuffs one of these, the small plastic squeaker inside can be dangerous if swallowed. Monitor the condition of your pup's toys carefully and get rid of any that have been chewed to the point of becoming potentially dangerous.

Be careful of natural bones, which have a tendency to splinter into sharp, dangerous pieces. Also be careful of rawhide, which after enough chewing can turn into pieces that are easy to swallow, and also watch out for the mushy mess it can turn into on your carpet.

LEAD

A nylon lead is probably the best option as it is the most resistant to puppy teeth should your pup take a liking to chewing on his lead. Of course, this is a habit that should be nipped in the bud, but if your pup likes to chew on his lead he has a very slim chance of being able to chew through the strong nylon. Nylon leads are

45

Choke collars should only be used for training and require expertise on the part of the owner.

DID YOU KNOW?

With a big variety of dog toys available, and so many that look like they would be a lot of fun for a dog, be careful in your selection. It is amazing what a set of puppy teeth can do to an innocent-looking toy, so, obviously, safety is a major consideration. Be sure to choose the most durable products that you can find. A retrieving breed like the Labrador Retriever will more often than not have something in its mouth. Hard nylon bones and toys are a safe bet, and many of them are offered in different scents and flavours that will be sure to capture your Labrador Retriever's attention. It is always fun to play a game of catch with your dog, and there are balls and flying discs that are specially made to withstand dog teeth.

also lightweight, which is good for a young Labrador Retriever who is just getting used to the idea of walking on a lead. For everyday walking and safety purposes, the nylon lead is a good choice. As your pup grows up and gets used to walking on the lead, and can do it politely, you may want to purchase a flexible lead, which allows you either to extend the length to give the dog a broader area to explore or to pull in the lead when you want to keep him close. Of course there are special leads for training purposes, and specially made leather harnesses for the working Labrador Retriever, but these are not necessary for routine walks. If your Labrador Retriever is especially strong or tends to pull on the lead, you may want to purchase something stronger, like a thicker leather lead.

COLLAR

Your pup should get used to wearing a collar all the time since you will want to attach his ID tags to his collar. Also, the lead and collar go hand in hand—you have to attach the lead to something! A lightweight nylon collar will be a good choice; make sure that it fits snugly enough so that the pup cannot wriggle out of it, but loose enough so that it will

not be uncomfortably tight around the pup's neck. You should be able to fit a finger in between the pup and the collar. It may take some time for your pup to get used to wearing the collar, but soon he will not even notice that it is there. Choke collars are made for training, but should only be used by an owner who knows exactly how to use it. If you use a stronger leather lead or a chain lead to walk your Labrador Retriever, you will need a stronger collar as well.

FOOD AND WATER BOWLS

Your pup will need two bowls, one for food and one for water. You may want two sets of bowls, one for inside and one for outside, depending on where the dog will be fed and where he will be spending most of his time. Stainless steel or sturdy plastic bowls are popular choices. Although plastic

Your local pet shop will have a variety of collars, harnesses, leads and combinations thereof. Be sure to get the correct size.

Pet shops offer a wide range of food and water bowls. Consider buying two sets... one for inside and one for outside.

Dog dishes and bowls are manufactured from plastic, pottery and stainless steel.

bowls are more chewable, dogs tend not to chew on the steel variety, which can also be sterilised. Some dog owners like to put their dogs' food and water bowls on a specially made elevated stand; this brings the food closer to the dog's level so he does not have to bend down as far, thus aiding his digestion and helping to guard against bloat or gastric torsion in deep-chested dogs. The most important thing is to buy sturdy bowls since, again, anything is in danger of being chewed by puppy teeth and you do not want your dog to be constantly chewing apart his bowl (for his safety and for your wallet!).

Always be sure your Lab has clean water available.

CLEANING SUPPLIES

A pup that is not housetrained means you will be doing a lot of cleaning until he is. Accidents will occur, which is okay for now because he does not know any better. All you can do is clean up any 'accidents'—old rags, towels, newspapers and a safe disinfectant are good to have on hand.

BEYOND THE BASICS

The items previously discussed are the bare necessities. You will find out what else you need as you go along—grooming supplies, flea/tick protection, baby gates to partition a room, etc.—these things will vary depending on your situation. It is just important that right away you have everything you need to feed and make your Labrador Retriever comfortable in his first few days at home.

PUPPY-PROOFING YOUR HOME

Aside from making sure that your Labrador Retriever will be comfortable in your home, you also have to make sure that your home is safe for your Labrador Retriever. This means taking precautions to make sure that your pup will not get into anything he should not get into and that there is nothing within his reach that may harm him should he sniff it, chew it, inspect it, etc. This probably seems obvious since, while you are primarily concerned with your pup's safety, at the same time you do not want your belongings to be ruined. Breakables should be placed out of reach if your dog is to have full run of the house. If he is to be limited to certain places within the house, keep any potentially dangerous items in the 'off-limits' areas. An electrical cord can pose a danger should the puppy decide to taste it—and who is going to convince a pup that it would not make a great chew toy? Cords should be kept from puppy's teeth and fastened tightly against the wall. If your dog is going to spend time in a crate, make sure that there is nothing near his crate

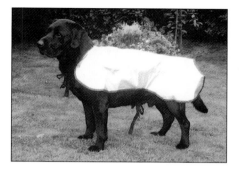

Yes—you can find rain capes for your Labrador Retriever.

cleaners and chemicals where the pup cannot get to them.

It is just as important to make sure that the outside of your home is safe. Of course

Your Labrador's proper care comes first.

that he can reach if he sticks his curious little nose or paws through the openings. And just as you would with a child, keep all household

your puppy should never be unsupervised, but a pup let loose in the garden will want to run and explore, and he should be granted that freedom. Do not let a fence give you a false sense of security; you would be surprised how crafty (and persistent) a dog can be in figuring out how to dig under and squeeze his way through small holes, or to jump or climb over a fence. The remedy is to make the fence high enough so that it really is impossible for your dog to get over it (about 3 metres should suffice), and well embedded into

A black Lab and a young friend make themselves comfortable.

the ground. Be sure to repair or secure any gaps in the fence. Check the fence periodically to ensure that it is in good shape and make repairs as needed; a very determined pup may return to the same spot to 'work on it' until he is able to get through.

FIRST TRIP TO THE VET

Okay, you have picked out your puppy, your home and family are ready, now all you have to do is pick your Labrador Retriever up from the breeder and the fun begins, right? Well…not so fast. Something else you need to prepare for is your pup's first trip to the veterinary surgeon. Perhaps the breeder can recommend someone in the area that specialises in Labrador Retrievers, or maybe you know some other Labrador Retriever owners who can suggest a good vet. Either way, you should have

A reputable breeder will guarantee that the puppy you buy is healthy. A novice may find it hard to define a problem just by looking at the puppy.

DID YOU KNOW?

Thoroughly puppy-proof your house before bringing your puppy home. Never use roach or rodent poisons in any area accessible to the puppy. Avoid the use of toilet bowl cleaners. Most dogs are born with toilet bowl sonar and will take a drink if the lid is left open. Also keep the trash secured and out of reach.

Scour your carport for potential puppy dangers. Remove weed killers, pesticides and antifreeze materials. Antifreeze is highly toxic and even a few drops can kill an adult dog.

Examine your lawn and garden landscaping before you bring your puppy home. Many varieties of plants have leaves, stems or flowers that are toxic if ingested. Ask your veterinarian for more information.

an appointment arranged for your pup before you pick him up; plan on taking him for a checkup within the first few days of bringing him home.

The pup's first visit will consist of an overall examination to make sure that the pup does not have any problems that are not apparent to the eye. The veterinary surgeon will also set up a schedule for the pup's vaccinations; the breeder will inform you of which ones the pup has already received and the vet can continue from there.

INTRODUCTION TO THE FAMILY

Everyone in the house will be excited about the puppy coming home and will want to pet him and play with him, but it is best to make the introduction low-key so as not to overwhelm the puppy. He is apprehensive already; it is the first time he has been separated from his mother and the breeder, and the ride to your home is likely the first time he has been in a car. The last thing you want to do is smother him, as this will only frighten him fur-

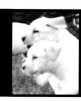

Written sales agreements from your breeder are not unusual.

ther. This is not to say that human contact is not extremely necessary at this stage, because this is the time when an instant connection between the pup and his human family is formed. Gentle petting and soothing words should help console him, as well as just putting him down and letting him explore on his own (under your watchful eye, of course).

The pup may approach family members or may busy himself with exploring for a while. Gradually, each person should spend some time with the pup, one at a time, crouching down to get as close to the pup's level as possible and letting him sniff their hands and petting him gently. He definitely needs human attention and he needs to be touched—this is how to form an immediate

Cloudy eyes and lack of enthusiasm are symptoms that must be evaluated by a veterinary surgeon.

bond. Just remember that the pup is experiencing a lot of things for the first time, all at the same time. There are new people, new noises, new smells, and new things to investigate; so be gentle, be affectionate and be as comforting as you can be.

dren and the less-than-happy cat. He's explored his area, his new bed, the garden and anywhere else he's been permitted. He's eaten his first meal at home and relieved himself in the proper place. He's heard lots of new sounds, smelled new friends and seen

You cannot tell if a Lab puppy will grow up to be a champion, but you can tell if certain undesirable physical characteristics will prevent him from being eligible for showing.

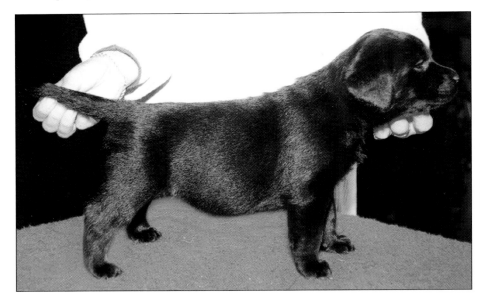

YOUR PUP'S FIRST NIGHT HOME

You have travelled home with your new charge safely in his basket or crate. He's been to the vet for a thorough checkover; he's been weighed, his papers examined; perhaps he's even been vaccinated and wormed as well. He's met the family, licked the whole family, including the excited chil-

more of the outside world than ever before.

That was the just the first day! He's exhausted and is ready for bed...or so you think!

It's puppy's first night and you are ready to say 'Good night'—keep in mind that this is puppy's first night ever to be sleeping alone. His dam and littermates are no longer at paw's length and he's a bit scared, cold and lonely. Be reassuring to your new family member. This is not the time to spoil him and give in to his inevitable whining.

Puppies whine. They whine to let the others know where they are and hopefully to get company out of it. Place

from his former homestead in his new bed so that he recognises the scent of his littermates. Others still advise placing a hot water bottle in his bed for warmth. This latter may be a good idea provided the pup doesn't attempt to suckle—he'll get good and wet

Do not place young Labs in unsafe positions. These puppies may be frightened of the height, or may injure themselves trying to get down.

your pup in his new bed or crate in his room and close the door. Mercifully, he will fall asleep without a peep. If the inevitable occurs, ignore the whining; he is fine. Be strong and keep his interest in mind. Do not allow your heart to become guilty and visit the pup. He will fall asleep.

Many breeders recommend placing a piece of bedding

and may not fall asleep so fast.

Puppy's first night can be somewhat stressful for the pup and his new family. Remember that you are setting the tone of nighttime at your house. Unless you want to play with your pup every evening at 10 p.m., midnight and 2 a.m., don't initiate the habit. Surely your family will thank you, and so will your pup!

PREVENTING PUPPY PROBLEMS

SOCIALISATION

Now that you have done all of the preparatory work and have helped your pup get accustomed to his new home and family, it is about time for you to have some fun! Socialising your Labrador Retriever pup gives you the opportunity to show off your new friend, and your pup gets to reap the benefits of being an adorable furry creature that people will adore, want to pet and, in general, think is absolutely precious!

Besides getting to know his new family, your puppy should be exposed to other people, animals and situations. This will help him become well adjusted as he grows up and less prone to being timid or fearful of the new things he will encounter. Your pup's

socialisation began at the breeder's, now it is your responsibility to continue. The socialisation he receives up until the age of 12 weeks is the most critical, as this is the time when he forms his impressions of the outside world. Lack of socialisation can manifest itself in fear and aggression as the dog grows up. He needs lots of human contact, affection, handling and exposure to other animals. Be careful during the eight-to-ten-week period, also known as the fear period. The interaction he receives during this time should be gentle and reassuring.

Once your pup has received his necessary vaccinations, feel free to take him out and about

DID YOU KNOW?

Thorough socialisation includes not only meeting new people but also being introduced to new experiences such as riding in the car, having his coat brushed, hearing the television, walking in a crowd—the list is endless. The more your pup experiences, and the more positive the experiences are, the less of a shock and the less scary it will be for your pup to encounter new things.

during this very formative stage will impact his attitude toward future encounters. A pup that has a bad experience with a child may grow up to be a dog that is shy around or aggressive toward children, and you want your dog to be comfortable around everyone.

Lab puppies are very curious and will investigate anything they can reach.

CONSISTENCY IN TRAINING
Dogs, being pack animals, naturally need a leader, or else they try to establish dominance in their packs. When you bring a dog into your family, who becomes the leader and who becomes the 'pack' are entirely up to you! Your pup's intuitive quest for dominance, coupled with the fact that it is nearly impossible to look at an adorable Labrador Retriever pup, with his 'puppy-dog' eyes and his too-

(on his lead, of course). Take him around the neighbourhood, take him on your daily errands, let people pet him, let him meet other dogs and pets, etc. Puppies do not have to try to make friends; there will be no shortage of people who will want to introduce themselves. Just make sure that you carefully supervise each meeting. If the neighbourhood children want to say hello, for example, that is great—children and pups most often make great companions. But sometimes an excited child can unintentionally handle a pup too roughly, or an overzealous pup can playfully nip a little too hard. You want to make socialisation experiences positive ones; what a pup learns

Your Labrador puppy needs you to be his leader.

big-for-his-head-still-floppy ears, and not cave in, give the pup almost an unfair advantage in getting the upper hand! And a pup will definitely test the waters to see what he can and cannot get away with. Do not give in to those pleading eyes—stand your ground when it comes to disciplining the pup and make sure that all family members do the same. It will only confuse the pup when Mother tells him to get off the couch when he is used to sitting up there with Father to watch the nightly news. Avoid discrepancies by having all members of the household decide on the rules before the pup even comes home...and be consistent in enforcing them! Early training shapes the dog's personality, so you cannot be unclear in what you expect.

COMMON PUPPY PROBLEMS

The best way to prevent problems is to be proactive in stopping an undesirable behaviour as soon as it starts. The old saying 'You can't teach an old dog new tricks'

Do not give in to pleading eyes!

does not necessarily hold true, but it is true that it is much easier to discourage bad behaviour in a young developing pup than to wait until the pup's bad behaviour becomes the adult dog's bad habit. There are some prob-

lems that are especially prevalent in puppies as they develop.

NIPPING

As puppies start to teethe, they feel the need to sink their teeth into anything...unfortunately that includes your fingers, arms, hair, toes...whatever happens to be available. You may find this behaviour cute for about the first five seconds...until you feel just how sharp those puppy teeth are. This is something you want to discourage immediately and consistently with a firm 'No!' (or whatever number of firm 'No's it takes for him to understand that you mean business) and replace your finger with an appropriate chew toy. While this behaviour is merely annoying when the dog is still young, it can become dangerous as your Labrador Retriever's adult teeth grow in and his jaws develop, if he thinks that it is okay to gnaw on human appendages. Although the Labrador is bred to have a 'soft' mouth, so as not to damage the game he retrieves, he can still cause a person great pain by nipping and biting.

CRYING/WHINING

Your pup will often cry, whine, whimper, howl or

Labrador Retrievers are beautiful puppies and they quickly learn that body language, especially facial expressions, will help them get their own way.

make some type of commotion when he is left alone. This is basically his way of calling out for attention, of calling out to make sure that you know he is there and that you have not forgotten about him. He feels insecure when he is left alone, for example, when you are out of the house and he is in his crate or when you are in another part of the house and he cannot see you. The noise he is making is an expression of the anxiety he feels at being alone, so he needs to be taught that being alone is okay. You are not actually training the dog to stop making noise, you are training him to feel comfortable when he is alone and thus removing the need for him to make the noise. This is where the crate filled with cosy blankets and a toy comes in handy. You want to know that he is safe when you are not there to supervise, and you know that he will be safe in his crate rather than roaming freely about the house. In order for the pup to stay in his crate without making a fuss, he needs to be comfortable in his crate. On that note, it is extremely important that the crate is never used as a form of punishment, or the pup will have a negative association with the crate.

Accustom the pup to the crate in short, gradually increasing time intervals in

Labrador Retriever puppies require proper training from the moment you bring them home. Do not tolerate nipping.

which you put him in the crate, maybe with a treat, and stay in the room with him. If he cries or makes a fuss, do not go to him, but stay in his sight. Gradually he will realise that staying in his crate is all right without your help, and it will not be so traumatic for him when you are not around. You may want to leave the radio on softly when you leave the house; the sound of human voices may be comforting to him.

DID YOU KNOW?

You will probably start feeding your Labrador Retriever pup the same food that he has been getting from the breeder; the breeder should give you a few days' supply to start you off. Although you should not give your pup too many treats, you will want to have puppy treats on hand for coaxing, training, rewards, etc. Be careful, though, as a small pup's calorie requirements are relatively low and a few treats can add up to almost a full day's worth of calories without the required nutrition.

With proper care and training, your cute, curious Lab puppy will grow into a beautiful, polite adult dog.

Internal Organs with Skeletal Structure

1. Esophagus
2. Lungs
3. Gall Bladder
4. Liver
5. Kidney
6. Stomach
7. Intestines
8. Urinary Bladder

Everyday Care of Your Labrador Retriever

DIETARY AND FEEDING CONSIDERATIONS

You have probably heard it a thousand times, you are what you eat. Believe it or not, it's very true. For dogs, they are what you feed them because they have little choice in the matter. Even those people who truly want to feed their dogs the best often cannot do so because they do not know which foods are best for their dog.

Dog foods are produced in three basic types: dried, semi-moist and canned or tinned. Dried foods are for the cost conscious

because they are much less expensive than semi-moist and canned. Dried foods contain the least fat and the most preservatives. Most tinned foods are 60–70-percent water, while semi-moist foods are so full of sugar that they are the least preferred by owners, though dogs welcome them (as does a child sweets).

Three stages of development must be considered when selecting a diet for your dog: the puppy stage, the mid-age or adult stage and the senior age or geriatric stage.

> **DID YOU KNOW?**
> Selecting the best dried food for your Labrador Retriever is extremely difficult.
>
> There are arguments among veterinary scientists as to the value of nutrient analyses (protein, fat, fibre, moisture, ash, cholesterol, minerals, etc.).
>
> All agree that feeding trials are what matters, but you also have to consider the individual Labrador Retriever and activity and age. It is probably most wise to depend upon your veterinary surgeon to recommend a diet for your dog. He can change the diet as the needs of your dog change.
>
> If your dog is fed a good dried food, it does not require supplements of meat or vegetables. Labrador Retrievers don't need variety in their diets. The same dried food every day suits them perfectly as long as it is nutritionally sound.

Your veterinary surgeon can help you determine which diet is best for your Lab puppy. The recommended diet will change as the dog grows.

Shiny coat and alert demeanour are indications of proper nutrition and good health.

PUPPY STAGE

Puppies have a natural instinct to suck milk from their mother's breasts. They should exhibit this behaviour the first day of their lives. If they don't suckle within a few hours, you should attempt to put them onto their mother's nipple. Their failure to feed means you have to feed them yourself under the advice and guidance of a veterinary surgeon. This will involve a baby bottle and a special formula. Their mother's milk is much better than any formula because it contains colostrum, a sort of antibiotic milk which protects puppies during the first eight to ten weeks of their lives.

Puppies should be allowed to nurse for six weeks and they should be slowly weaned away from their mother by introducing

small portions of tinned meat after they are about one month old.

By the time they are eight weeks old, they should be completely weaned and fed solely a puppy dried food. During this weaning period, their diet is most important as the puppy grows fastest during its first year of life. Growth foods can be recommended by your veterinary surgeon and the puppy should be kept on this diet for up to 18 months.

Unless there is a problem, the puppy should nurse from its mother. Small bottles and formulas exist for feeding puppies that cannot suckle their mother.

Even if each dog has his own bowl, it does not mean that one will not try to steal from someone else's bowl.

Puppy diets should be balanced for your dog's needs and supplements of vitamins, minerals and protein should not be necessary.

ADULT DIETS

A dog is considered an adult when it has stopped growing. The growth is in height and/or length. Do not consider the dog's weight when the decision is

Labs must have balanced diets at every age.

made to switch from a puppy diet to a maintenance diet. Again you should rely upon your veterinary surgeon to recommend an acceptable maintenance diet. Major dog food manufacturers specialise in this type of food and it is just necessary for you to select the one best suited to your dog's needs. Active dogs may have different requirements than sedate dogs.

A Labrador Retriever reaches adulthood at about two years of age, though some dogs fully mature at 16 months, while others may take up to three years.

DIETS FOR SENIOR DOGS

As dogs get older, their metabolism changes. The older dog usu-

Dogs are considered to be adults when they stop growing. Adult dogs should be fed a maintenance, rather than a puppy growth, food.

ally exercises less, moves more slowly and sleeps more. This change in lifestyle and physiological performance requires a change in diet. Since these changes take place slowly, they might not be recognisable. What is easily recognisable is weight gain. By continually feeding your dog an adult maintenance diet when it is slowing down metabolically, your dog will gain weight. Obesity in an older dog compounds the health problems that already accompany old age.

As your dog gets older, few of its organs function up to par. The kidneys slow down and the intestines become less efficient. These age-related factors are best handled with a change in diet and a change in feeding schedule to give smaller portions that are more easily digested.

There is no single best diet for every older dog. While many

What are you feeding your dog?

NUTRIENTS:
1.3% Calcium
1.6% Fatty Acids
4.6% Crude Fibre
11% Moisture
14% Crude Fat
22% Crude Protein

UNDOCUMENTED
45.5% ? ? ?

*Read the label
on your dog food.
Most manufacturers
merely advise you of
50-55% of the contents,
leaving the other
45% in doubt.*

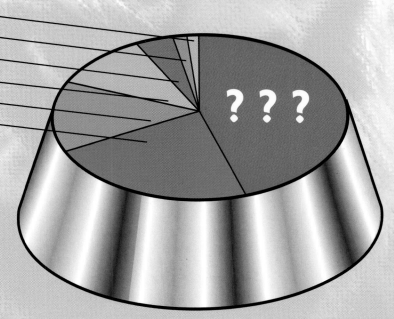

While adult diets are necessary for the mature Lab, active dogs have different needs than more sedentary dogs.

dogs do well on light or senior diets, other dogs do better on puppy diets or other special premium diets such as lamb and rice.

Be sensitive to your senior Labrador Retriever's diet and this will help control other problems that may arise with your old friend.

WATER

Just as your dog needs proper nutrition from his food, water is an essential 'nutrient' as well. Water keeps the dog's body properly hydrated and promotes normal function of the body's systems. During housebreaking it is necessary to keep an eye on how much water your Labrador Retriever is drinking, but once he is reliably trained he should have

access to clean fresh water at all times. Make sure that the dog's water bowl is clean, and change the water often.

EXERCISE

All dogs require some form of exercise, regardless of breed. A

sedentary lifestyle is as harmful to a dog as it is to a person. The Labrador Retriever happens to be an active breed that requires more exercise than, say, an English Bulldog, but you don't have to be a weightlifter or marathon runner to provide your dog with the exercise he needs. Regular walks, play sessions in the garden, or letting the dog run free in the garden under your supervision are all sufficient forms of exercise for the Labrador Retriever. For those who are more ambitious, you will find that your Labrador Retriever will be able to keep up with you on extra long walks or the morning run. Not only is exercise essential to

Every animal, whether dog, cat or human, requires water regularly. The water for your Lab must be clean, fresh and changed often.

keep the dog's body fit, it is essential to his mental well-being. A bored dog will find something to do, which often manifests itself in some type

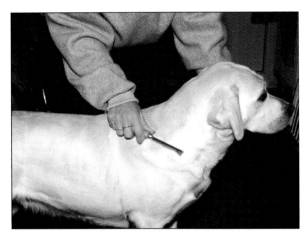

of destructive behaviour. In this sense, it is essential for the owner's mental well-being as well!

Labrador Retrievers require minimal grooming, but they should be combed (with a metal comb) and/or brushed on a daily basis.

GROOMING
BRUSHING
A slicker brush, pin brush or metal comb can be used for regular routine brushing. Daily brushing is effective for removing dead hair and stimulating the dog's natural oils to add shine and a healthy look to the coat. Your Labrador Retriever is not a breed that needs excessive grooming, but his coat needs to be brushed daily as part of routine maintenance. Daily brushing will minimise

tangles and matts, get rid of dust and dandruff, and remove any dead hair. Regular grooming sessions are also a good way to spend time with your dog. Many dogs grow to like the feel of being brushed and will enjoy the daily routine.

BATHING
Dogs do not need to be bathed as often as humans, but regular bathing is essential for healthy skin and a healthy, shiny coat. Again, like most anything, if you accustom your pup to being bathed as a puppy, it will be second nature by the time he grows up. You want your dog to be at ease in the bath or else it could end up a wet, soapy, messy ordeal for both of you!

Brush your Labrador Retriever thoroughly before wetting his coat. This will get rid of most matts and tangles, which are harder to remove when the coat is wet. Make sure that your dog has a good non-slip surface to stand on. Begin by wetting the dog's coat. A shower or hose attachment is necessary for thoroughly wetting and rinsing the coat. Check the water temperature to make sure that it is neither too hot nor too cold.

Next, apply shampoo to the dog's coat and work it into a good lather. You should purchase a shampoo that is made for dogs; do not use a product

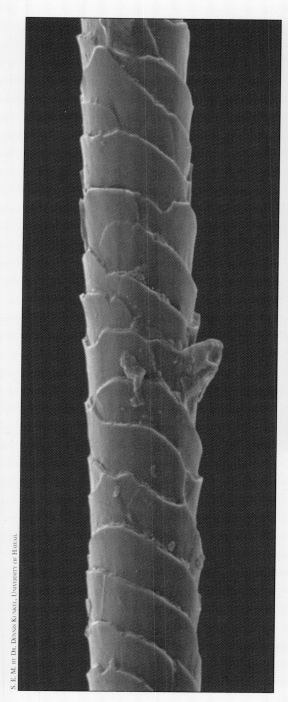

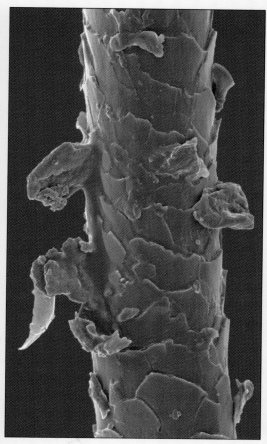

Scanning electron micrograph images of two hairs from a black Labrador Retriever. The hair to the left is a normal, healthy hair to which a few dead skin cells are clinging (part of the dandruff). The cuticle (outer covering) is normal and uniform. The hair shown above is a sick or injured hair as evidenced by the damaged, unkempt cuticle. These historical photos, the first ever having been done of Lab hairs on an electron microscope, were accomplished by Dr. Dennis Kunkel at the University of Hawaii, specifically for this book.

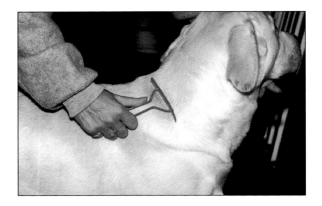

A wide-tooth metal rake in use on a Labrador Retriever.

EAR CLEANING

The ears should be kept clean and any excess hair inside the ear should be trimmed. Ears can be cleaned with a cotton wipe and special cleaner or ear powder made especially for dogs. Be on the lookout for any signs of infection or ear mite infestation. If your Labrador Retriever has been shaking his head or scratching at his ears frequently, this usually indicates a problem. If his ears have an unusual odour, this is a sure sign of mite infestation or infection, and a signal to have his ears checked by the veterinary surgeon.

made for human hair. Wash the head last; you do not want shampoo to drip into the dog's eyes while you are washing the rest of his body. Work the shampoo all the way down to the skin. You can use this opportunity to check the skin for any bumps, bites or other abnormalities. Do not neglect any area of the body—get all of the hard-to-reach places.

Once the dog has been thoroughly shampooed, he requires an equally thorough rinsing. Shampoo left in the coat can be irritating to the skin. Protect his eyes from the shampoo by shielding them with your hand and directing the flow of water in the opposite direction. You should also avoid getting water in the ear canal. Be prepared for your dog to shake out his coat— you might want to stand back, but make sure you have a hold on the dog to keep him from running through the house.

DID YOU KNOW?

How much grooming equipment you purchase will depend on how much grooming you are going to do. Here are some of the basics:

• Natural bristle brush
• Slicker brush
• Metal comb
• Wide-tooth metal rake
• Scissors
• Blaster
• Electric clippers
• Rubber mat
• Dog shampoo
• Spray hose attachment
• Ear cleaner
• Cotton wipes
• Heavy towels
• Nail clippers

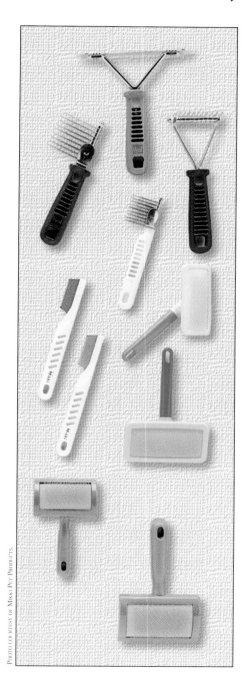

NAIL CLIPPING

Your Labrador Retriever should be accustomed to having his nails trimmed at an early age, since it will be part of your maintenance routine throughout his life. Not only does it look nicer, but a dog with long nails can cause injury if he jumps up or if he scratches someone unintentionally. Also, a long nail has a better chance of ripping and bleeding, or

Your local pet shop will have a variety of useful grooming tools in the form of brushes, rakes and combs.

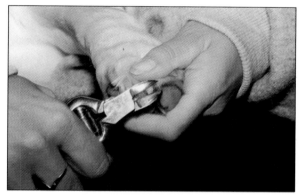

causing the feet to spread. A good rule of thumb is that if you can hear your dog's nails clicking on the floor when he walks, his nails are too long.

Before you start cutting, make sure you can identify the 'quick' in each nail. The quick is a blood vessel that runs through the centre of each nail and grows rather close to the end. It will bleed if accidentally cut, which will be quite painful for the dog as it con-

Cutting your Lab's nails requires care that the quick is not severed. Special nail cutters are used for dog's nails.

71

tains nerve endings. Keep some type of clotting agent on hand, such as a styptic pencil or styptic powder (the type used for

BREED-SPECIFIC GROOMING CONSIDERATIONS

Labrador Retrievers do not require elaborate haircuts or a lot of finishing work. Basically, the main goal in grooming the Labrador Retriever is to keep the dog's coat looking nice and in good health. During moulting season in the spring you will need to pay a little more attention to his coat, but a vigorous brushing will suffice to loosen much of the dead hair in the undercoat. Follow up with a metal comb to remove the hair that is being cast off.

NEVER travel with your dog(s) freely roaming around your automobile. It is dangerous for both you and the dogs.

shaving). This will stop the bleeding quickly when applied to the end of the cut nail. Do not panic if this happens, just stop the bleeding and talk soothingly to your dog. Once he has calmed down, move on to the next nail. It is better to clip a little at a time, particularly with black-nailed dogs.

Hold your pup steady as you begin trimming his nails; you do not want him to make any sudden movements or run away. Talk to him soothingly and stroke his fur as you clip. Holding his foot in your hand, simply take off the end of each nail in one quick clip. You can purchase nail clippers that are specially made for dogs; you can probably find them wherever you buy pet or grooming supplies.

Some owners like to emphasize the otter-like look of the Labrador's tail by trimming it to give it a blunt point. Spray-on coat gloss is another optional grooming tool; this will give the Labrador's short, dense coat a sleek sheen. An

extra-shiny coat looks especially nice on black dogs.

TRAVELLING WITH YOUR DOG

CAR TRAVEL

You should accustom your
Labrador Retriever to riding in
a car at an early age. You may
or may not often take him in
the car, but at the very least he
will need to go to the vet and
you do not want these trips to
be traumatic for the dog or a
big hassle for you. The safest
way for a dog to ride in the car
is in his crate. If he uses a
fibreglass crate in the house,
you can use the same crate for
travel. If you have a wire crate
in the house, consider purchasing an appropriately sized
fibreglass or wooden crate for
travelling. Wire crates can be
used for travel, but fibreglass
or wooden crates are safer.

Put the pup in the crate and
see how he reacts. If he seems
uneasy, you can have a passen-
ger hold him on his lap while
you drive. Another option is a
specially made safety harness
for dogs, which straps the dog
in much like a seat belt. Do not
let the dog roam loose in the
vehicle—this is very dangerous! If you should stop short,
your dog can be thrown and
injured. If the dog starts climbing on you and pestering you
while you are driving, you will

*An appro-
priately
sized crate
will keep
your Lab
safe while
travelling.*

not be able to concentrate on
the road. It is an unsafe situation for everyone—human and
canine.

For long trips, be prepared
to stop to let the dog relieve
himself. Bring along whatever
you need to clean up after him.
You should bring along some
old towels and rags, should he
have an accident in the car or
become carsick.

AIR TRAVEL

Whilst it is possible to take a
dog on a flight within Britain,
this is fairly unusual and
advance permission is always
required. The dog will be
required to travel in a fibreglass crate and you should

DID YOU KNOW?

The most extensive travel you do with
your dog may be limited to trips to
the veterinary surgeon's office—or you
may decide to bring him along for
long distances when the family goes
on holiday. Whichever the case, it is
important to consider your dog's safety while travelling.

DID YOU KNOW?

For international travel you will have to make arrangements well in advance (perhaps months), as countries' regulations pertaining to bringing in animals differ. There may be special health certificates and/or vaccinations that your dog will need before taking the trip, sometimes this has to be done within a certain time frame. In rabies-free countries, you will need to bring proof of the dog's rabies vaccination and there may be a quarantine period upon arrival.

always check in advance with the airline regarding specific requirements. You may be able to use your own crate or the airline can usually supply one. To help the dog be at ease, put one of his favourite toys in the crate with him. Do not feed the dog for at least six hours before the trip to minimise his need to relieve himself. However, certain regulations specify that water must always be made available to the dog in the crate.

Make sure your dog is properly identified and that your contact information appears on his ID tags and on his crate. Animals travel in a different area of the plane than human passengers, and, although transporting animals is routine for many airlines, there is always that slight risk of getting separated from your dog.

BOARDING

So you want to take a family holiday—and you want to include all members of the family. You would probably make arrangements for accommodations ahead of time anyway, but this is especially important when travelling with a dog. You do not want to make an overnight stop at the only place around for miles to find out that they do not allow dogs. Also, you do not want to reserve a place for your family without mentioning that you are bringing a dog, because if it is against their policy you may not have a place to stay.

Alternatively, if you are travelling and choose not to bring your

DID YOU KNOW?

If your dog gets lost, he is not able to ask for directions home.

Identification tags fastened to the collar give important information— the dog's name, the owner's name, the owner's address and a telephone number where the owner can be reached. This makes it easy for whoever finds the dog to contact the owner and arrange to have the dog returned. An added advantage is that a person will be more likely to approach a lost dog who has ID tags on his collar; it tells the person that this is somebody's pet rather than a stray. This is the easiest and fastest method of identification provided that the tags stay on the collar and the collar stays on the dog.

Labrador Retriever, you will have to make arrangements for him while you are away. Some options are to bring him to a neighbour's house to stay while you are gone, to have a trusted neighbour stop by often or stay at your house, or bring your dog to a reputable boarding kennel. If you choose to board him at a kennel, you should stop by to see the facility and where the dogs are kept to make sure that it is clean. Talk to some of the employees and see how they treat the dogs—do they spend time with the dogs, play with them, exercise them, etc.? You know that your Labrador Retriever will not be happy unless he gets regular activity. Also find out the kennel's policy on vaccinations and what they require. This is for all of the dogs' safety, since when dogs are kept together, there is a greater risk of diseases being passed from dog to dog. Most facilities require the owner to provide current vaccination documentation.

IDENTIFICATION

Your Labrador Retriever is your valued companion and friend. That is why you always keep a close eye on him and you have made sure that he cannot escape from the garden or wriggle out of his collar and run away from you. However, accidents can happen and there may come a time when your dog unexpectedly gets separated from you. If this unfortunate event should occur, the first thing on your mind will be finding him. Proper identification will increase the chances of his being returned to you safely and quickly.

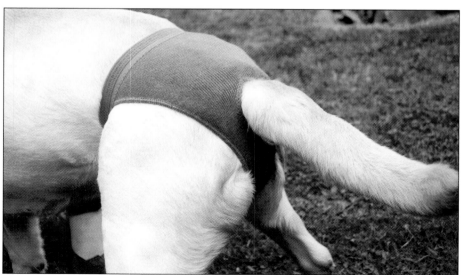

Your local pet shop will have many items, which are too numerous to mention in a book. An example is the special panties that are used for bitches in heat. It protects them from staining as well as having an unplanned mating.

Housebreaking and Training Your Labrador Retriever

Living with an untrained dog is a lot like owning a piano that you do not know how to play—it is a nice object to look at but it does not do much more than that to bring you pleasure. Now try taking piano lessons and suddenly the piano comes alive and brings forth magical sounds and rhythms that set your heart singing and your body swaying.

The same is true with your Labrador Retriever. At first you enjoy seeing him around the house. He does not do much with

Much of the Lab's popularity stems from his trainability and inherent good nature.

you other than to need food, water and exercise. Come to think of it, he does not bring you much joy, either. He is a big responsibility with a very small return. And often, he develops unacceptable behaviours that annoy and/or infuriate you to say nothing of bad habits that may end up costing you great sums of money. Not a good thing!

Now train your Labrador Retriever. Enrol in an obedience class. Teach him good manners as you learn how and why he behaves the way he does. Find out how to communicate with your dog and how to recognise and understand his communications with you. Suddenly the dog takes on a new role in your life—he is smart, interesting, well behaved and fun to be with, and he demonstrates his bond of devotion to you daily. In other words, your Labrador Retriever does wonders for your ego because he constantly reminds you that you are not only his leader, you are his hero! Miraculous things have happened—you have a wonderful dog (even your family and friends have noticed the transformation!) and you feel good about yourself.

Those involved with teaching dog obedience and counselling owners about their dogs' behaviour have discovered some interesting facts about dog ownership. For example, training dogs when they are puppies results in the highest rate of success in developing well-mannered and well-adjusted adult dogs. Training an older dog, say from six months to six years of age, can produce almost equal results providing that the owner accepts the dog's slower rate of learning capability and is willing to work patiently to help the dog succeed at developing to his fullest potential. Unfortunately, the patience factor is what many owners of untrained adult dogs lack, so they do not persist until their dogs are successful at learning particular behaviours.

Training a puppy, for example, aged 8 to 16 weeks (20 weeks at the most) is like working with a dry sponge in a pool of water. The pup soaks up whatever you show him and constantly looks for more things to do and learn. At this early age, his body is not yet producing hormones, and therein lies the reason for such a high rate of success. Without hormones, he is focused on his owners and not particularly interested in investigating other places, dogs, people, etc. You are his leader; his provider of food, water, shelter and security. Therefore, he latches onto you and wants to stay close. He will usually follow you from room to room, will not let you out of his sight when you are outdoors with him, and respond in like manner to the people and animals you encounter.

Puppies are most trainable between 2–4 months old.

If, for example, you greet a friend warmly, he will be happy to greet the person as well. If, however, you are hesitant, even anxious, about the approach of a stranger, he will respond accordingly.

Once the puppy begins to produce hormones, his natural curiosity emerges and he begins to investigate the world around him. It is at that time when you may notice that the untrained dog begins to wander away from you and even ignore your commands to stay close. When this behaviour becomes a problem, the owner has two choices: get rid of the dog or train him. It is strongly urged that you choose the latter option.

Occasionally there are no classes available within a reasonable distance from the owner's home. Sometimes there are classes available but the tuition is too costly. Whatever the circumstances, the solution to the problem of lack of lesson availability lies within the pages of this book.

This chapter is devoted to helping you train your Labrador Retriever at home. If the recommended procedures are followed faithfully, you may expect positive results that will prove rewarding to both you and your dog.

Whether your Labrador Retriever is a puppy or a mature adult, the methods of teaching and the techniques we use in training basic behaviours are the same. After all, no dog, whether puppy or adult, likes harsh or inhumane methods. All creatures, however, respond favourably to gentle motivational methods and sincere praise and encouragement. Now let us get started.

HOUSEBREAKING

You can train a puppy to relieve itself wherever you choose. For example, city dwellers often train their puppies to relieve themselves in the gutter because large plots of grass are not readily available. Suburbanites, on the other hand, usually have gardens to accommodate their dogs' needs.

Outdoor training includes such surfaces as grass, dirt and cement. Indoor training usually means training your dog to newspaper.

When deciding on the surface and location that you will want your Labrador Retriever to use, be sure it is going to be permanent. Training your dog to grass and then changing your mind two months later is extremely difficult for both dog and owner.

Next, choose the command you will use each and every time you want your puppy to void. 'Go hurry up' and 'Toilet' are examples of commands commonly used by dog owners.

Get in the habit of asking the puppy, 'Do you want to go hurry up?' (or whatever your chosen relief command is) before you take him out. That way, when he becomes an adult, you will be able to determine if he wants to go out when you ask him. A confirmation will be signs of interest, wagging his tail, watching you intently, going to the door, etc.

PUPPY'S NEEDS

Puppy needs to relieve himself after play periods, after each meal, after he has been sleeping and any time he indicates that he is looking for a place to urinate or defecate.

The urinary and intestinal tract muscles of very young puppies are not fully developed. Therefore, like human babies, puppies need to relieve themselves frequently.

Take your puppy out often—every hour for an eight-week-old, for example. The older the puppy, the less often he will need to relieve himself. Finally, as a mature healthy adult, he will require only three to five relief trips per day.

HOUSING

Since the types of housing and control you provide for your puppy has a direct relationship on the success of housetraining, we consider the various aspects of both before we begin training.

Bringing a new puppy home and turning him loose in your house can be compared to turning a child loose in a sports arena and telling the child that the place is all his! The sheer enormity of the place would be too much for him to handle.

Instead, offer the puppy clearly defined areas where he can play, sleep, eat and live. A room of the house where the family

DID YOU KNOW?

A basic obedience beginner's class usually lasts for six to eight weeks. Dog and owner attend an hour-long lesson once a week and practise for a few minutes, several times a day, each day at home. If done properly, the whole procedure will result in a well-mannered dog and an owner who delights in living with a pet that is eager to please and enjoys doing things with his owner.

gathers is the most obvious choice. Puppies are social animals and need to feel a part of the pack right from the start. Hearing your voice, watching you while you are doing things and smelling you nearby are all positive reinforcers that he is now a member of your pack. Usually a family room, the kitchen or a nearby adjoining breakfast nook is ideal for providing safety and security for both puppy and owner.

Within that room there should be a smaller area which the puppy can call his own. A cubbyhole, a wire or fibreglass dog crate or a fenced (not boarded!) corner from which he can view the activities of his new family will be fine. The size of the area or crate is the key factor here. The area must be large enough for the puppy to lay down and stretch out as well as stand up without rubbing his head on the top, yet small enough so that he cannot relieve himself at one end and sleep at the other without coming into contact with his droppings.

Dogs are, by nature, clean animals and will not remain close to their relief areas unless forced to do so. In those cases, they then become dirty dogs and usually remain that way for life.

The crate or cubby should be lined with a clean towel and offer one toy, no more. Do not put food or water in the crate, as eating and drinking will activate his digestive processes and ultimately defeat your purpose as well as make the puppy very uncomfortable as he attempts to 'hold it.'

CONTROL

By control, we mean helping the puppy to create a lifestyle pattern that will be compatible to that of his human pack (YOU!). Just as we guide little children to learn our way of life, we must show the puppy when it is time to play, eat, sleep, exercise and even entertain himself.

Your puppy should always sleep in his crate. He should also learn that, during times of household confusion and excessive human activity such as at breakfast when family members are preparing for the day, he can play by himself in relative safety and comfort in his crate. Each time you leave the puppy alone, he should be crated. Puppies are chewers. They cannot tell the difference between lamp cords, television wires, shoes, table legs, etc. Chewing into a television wire, for example, can be fatal to the puppy while a shorted wire can start a fire in the house.

If the puppy chews on the arm of the chair when he is alone, you will probably discipline him angrily when you get home. Thus, he makes the association that your coming home means he is going to be hit or punished. (He will not remember chewing up the chair and is incapable of making the association of the discipline with his naughty deed.)

Other times of excitement, such as family parties, etc., can be fun for the puppy providing he can view the activities from the security of his crate. He is not

Your Lab must be trained to consider his crate as his castle.

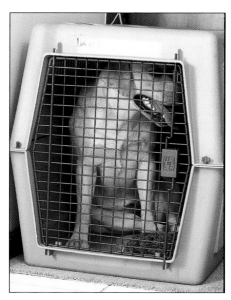

underfoot and he is not being fed all sorts of titbits that will probably cause him stomach distress, yet he still feels a part of the fun.

SCHEDULE

As stated earlier, a puppy should be taken to his relief area each time he is released from his crate, after meals, after a play session, when he first awakens in the morning (at age 8 weeks, this can mean 5 a.m.!) and whenever he indicates by circling or sniffing busily that he needs to urinate or defecate. For a puppy less than ten weeks of age, a routine of tak-

---

DID YOU KNOW?

Success that comes by luck is usually happenstance and frequently short lived. Success that comes by well-thought-out proven methods is often more easily achieved and permanent. This is the Success Method. It is designed to give you, the puppy owner, a simple yet proven way to help your Labrador puppy develop clean living habits and a feeling of security in his new environment.

---

ing him out every hour is necessary. As the puppy grows, he will be able to wait for longer periods of time.

Keep trips to his relief area short. Stay no more than five or six minutes and then return to the house. If he goes during that time, praise him lavishly and take him

indoors immediately. If he does not, but he has an accident when you go back indoors, pick him up immediately, say 'No! No!' and return to his relief area. Wait a

Crate training is recommended for most Labs.

few minutes, then return to the house again. NEVER hit a puppy or rub his face in urine or excrement when he has an accident!

Once indoors, put the puppy in his crate until you have had time to clean up his accident. Then release him to the family area and watch him more closely than before. Chances are, his accident was a result of your not picking up his signal or waiting too long before offering him the opportunity to relieve himself. NEVER hold a grudge against the puppy for accidents.

Let the puppy learn that going outdoors means it is time to relieve himself, not play. Once trained, he will be able to play indoors and out and still differentiate between the times for play versus the times for relief.

Help him develop regular hours for naps, being alone, playing by himself and just resting, all in his crate. Encourage him to entertain himself while you are

81

Canine Development Schedule

It is important to understand how and at what age a puppy develops into adulthood.
If you are a puppy owner, consult the following Canine Development Schedule to determine
the stage of development your Labrador Retriever puppy is currently experiencing.
This knowledge will help you as you work with the puppy in the weeks and months ahead.

Period	Age	Characteristics
FIRST TO THIRD	**BIRTH TO SEVEN WEEKS**	Puppy needs food, sleep and warmth, and responds to simple and gentle touching. Needs mother for security and disciplining. Needs littermates for learning and interacting with other dogs. Pup learns to function within a pack and learns pack order of dominance. Begin socialising with adults and children for short periods. Begins to become aware of its environment.
FOURTH	**EIGHT TO TWELVE WEEKS**	Brain is fully developed. Needs socialising with outside world. Remove from mother and littermates. Needs to change from canine pack to human pack. Human dominance necessary. Fear period occurs between 8 and 16 weeks. Avoid fright and pain.
FIFTH	**THIRTEEN TO SIXTEEN WEEKS**	Training and formal obedience should begin. Less association with other dogs, more with people, places, situations. Period will pass easily if you remember this is pup's change-to-adolescence time. Be firm and fair. Flight instinct prominent. Permissiveness and over-disciplining can do permanent damage. Praise for good behaviour.
JUVENILE	**FOUR TO EIGHT MONTHS**	Another fear period about 7 to 8 months of age. It passes quickly, but be cautious of fright and pain. Sexual maturity reached. Dominant traits established. Dog should understand sit, down, come and stay by now.

NOTE: THESE ARE APPROXIMATE TIME FRAMES. ALLOW FOR INDIVIDUAL DIFFERENCES IN PUPPIES.

DID YOU KNOW?

By providing sleeping and resting quarters that fit the dog, and offering frequent opportunities to relieve himself outside his quarters, the puppy quickly learns that the outdoors (or the newspaper if you are training him to paper) is the place to go when he needs to urinate or defecate. It also reinforces his innate desire to keep his sleeping quarters clean. This, in turn, helps develop the muscle control that will eventually produce a dog with clean living habits.

busy with your activities. Let him learn that having you near is comforting, but it is not your main purpose in life to provide him with undivided attention.

Each time you put a puppy in his crate tell him, 'Crate time!' (or whatever command you choose). Soon, he will run to his crate when he hears you say those words.

In the beginning of his training, do not leave him in his crate for prolonged periods of time except during the night when everyone is sleeping. Make his experience with his crate a

THE SUCCESS METHOD
6 Steps to Successful Crate Training

1 Tell the puppy 'Crate time!' and place him in the crate with a small treat (a piece of cheese or half of a biscuit). Let him stay in the crate for five minutes while you are in the same room. Then release him and praise lavishly. Never release him when he is fussing. Wait until he is quiet before you let him out.

2 Repeat Step 1 several times a day.

3 The next day, place the puppy in the crate as before. Let him stay there for ten minutes. Do this several times.

4 Continue building time in five-minute increments until the puppy

stays in his crate for 30 minutes with you in the room. Always take him to his relief area after prolonged periods in his crate.

5 Now go back to Step 1 and let the puppy stay in his crate for five minutes, this time while you are out of the room.

6 Once again, build crate time in five-minute increments with you out of the room. When the puppy will stay willingly in his crate (he may even fall asleep!) for 30 minutes with you out of the room, he will be ready to stay in it for several hours at a time.

DID YOU KNOW?

Never line your pup's sleeping area with newspaper. Puppy litters are usually raised on newspaper and, once in your home, the puppy will immediately associate newspaper with voiding. Never put newspaper on any floor while housetraining, as this will only confuse the puppy. If you are paper-training him, use paper in his designated relief area ONLY. Finally, restrict water intake after evening meals. Offer a few licks at a time—never let a young puppy gulp water after meals.

In conclusion, a few key elements are really all you need for a successful house and crate training method—consistency, frequency, praise, control and supervision. By following these procedures with a normal, healthy puppy, you and the puppy will soon be past the stage of 'accidents' and ready to move on to a full and rewarding life together.

ROLES OF DISCIPLINE, REWARD AND PUNISHMENT

Discipline, training one to act in accordance with rules, brings order

DID YOU KNOW?

Mealtime should be a peaceful time for your Labrador. Pick a relatively secluded, yet not isolated, spot (like a corner of the kitchen) for your Lab and feed him there every time. He should be able to eat undisturbed; do not let children get into his food bowl. You do not want your dog to develop a tendency toward food guarding.

Dogs need discipline in all situations, including behaving properly on the lead and around other dogs.

pleasant one and, as an adult, he will love his crate and willingly stay in it for several hours. There are millions of people who go to work every day and leave their adult dogs crated while they are away. The dogs accept this as their lifestyle and look forward to 'crate time.'

Crate training provides safety for you, the puppy and the home. It also provides the puppy with a feeling of security, and that helps the puppy achieve self-confidence and clean habits.

Remember that one of the primary ingredients in housetraining your puppy is control. Regardless of your lifestyle, there will always be occasions when you will need to have a place where your dog can stay and be happy and safe. Crate training is the answer for now and in the future.

to life. It is as simple as that. Without discipline, particularly in a group society, chaos reigns supreme and the group will eventually perish. Humans and canines are social animals and need some form of discipline in order to function effectively. They must procure food, protect their home base and their young and reproduce to keep the species going.

If there were no discipline in the lives of social animals, they would eventually die from starvation and/or predation by other stronger animals.

In the case of domestic canines, dogs need discipline in their lives in order to understand how their pack (you and other family members) functions and how they must act in order to survive.

Occasionally, and hopefully infrequently, dogs need to be punished.

DID YOU KNOW?

Most of all, be consistent. Always take your dog to the same location, always use the same command, and always have him on lead when he is in his relief area, unless a fenced-in garden is available.

By following the Success Method, your Labrador Retriever puppy will be completely housetrained by the time his muscle and brain development reach maturity. Keep in mind that small breeds usually mature faster than large breeds, even though large breeds like the Labrador Retriever grow rapidly, but all puppies should be trained by six months of age.

A large humane society in a highly populated area recently surveyed dog owners regarding their satisfaction with their relationships with their dogs. People who had trained their dogs were 75 percent more satisfied with their pets than those who had never trained their dogs.

Dr. Edward Thorndike, a psychologist, established *Thorndike's Theory of Learning*, which states that a behaviour that results in a pleasant event tends to be repeated. A behaviour that results in an unpleasant event tends not to be repeated. It is this theory on which training methods are based today. For example, if you manipulate a dog to perform a specific behaviour and reward him for doing it, he is likely to do it again because he enjoyed the end result.

Pet shops offer training collars and harnesses.

Occasionally, punishment, a penalty inflicted for an offence, is necessary. The best type of punishment often comes from an outside source. For example, a child is told not to touch the stove because he may get burned. He disobeys and touches the stove. In doing so, he receives a burn. From that time on, he respects the heat of the stove and avoids contact with it. Therefore, a behaviour that results in an unpleasant event tends not to be repeated.

A good example of a dog learning the hard way is the dog who chases the house cat. He is told many times to leave the cat alone, yet he persists in teasing the cat. Then, one day he begins chasing the cat but the cat turns and swipes a claw across the dog's face, leaving him with a painful gash on his nose. The final result is that the dog stops chasing the cat.

TRAINING EQUIPMENT
COLLAR
A simple buckle collar is fine for most dogs. One who pulls mightily on the leash may require a chain choker collar. Only in the most severe cases of a dog being totally out of control is it recommended to use a prong or pinch collar, and in this case only if the owner has been instructed in the proper use of such equipment. In some areas, such as the United Kingdom, these types of collars are not allowed.

LEAD
A 1- to 2-metre lead is recommended, preferably made of leather, nylon or heavy cloth. A chain lead is not recommended, as many dog owners find that the chain cuts into their hands and that switching the lead back and forth frequently between their hands is painful.

TREATS
Have a bag of treats on hand. Something nutritious and easy to swallow works best; use a soft treat, a chunk of cheese or a piece of cooked chicken rather than a dry biscuit. By the time the dog gets done chewing a dry treat, he will forget why he is being rewarded in the first place! Using food rewards will not teach a dog to beg at the table—the only way to teach a dog to beg at the table is to give him food from the table. In

training, rewarding the dog with a food treat away from the table will help him associate praise and the treats with learning new behaviours that obviously please his owner.

TRAINING BEGINS: ASK THE DOG A QUESTION

In order to teach your dog anything, you must first get his attention. After all, he cannot learn anything if he is looking away from you with his mind on something else.

To get his attention, ask him, 'School?' and immediately walk over to him and give him a treat as you tell him 'Good dog.' Wait a minute or two and repeat the routine, this time with a treat in your hand as you approach the dog to within a foot of him. Do not go directly to him, but stop about a foot short of him and hold out the treat as you ask, 'School?' He will see you approaching with a treat in your hand and most likely begin walking toward you. As you meet, give him the treat and praise again.

The third time, ask the question, have a treat in your hand and walk only a short distance toward the dog so that he must walk almost all the way to you. As he reaches you, give him the treat and praise again.

By this time, the dog will probably be getting the idea that if he pays attention to you, especially when you ask that question, it will pay off in treats and fun activities for him. In other words, he learns that 'school' means doing fun things with you that result in treats and positive attention for him.

Remember that the dog does not understand your verbal language, he only recognises sounds. Your question translates to a series of sounds for him, and those sounds become the signal to go to you and pay attention; if he does, he will get to interact with you plus receive treats and praise.

THE BASIC COMMANDS
TEACHING SIT

Now that you have the dog's attention, hold the lead in your left hand and the food treat in your right. Place your food hand at the dog's nose and let him lick the treat but not take it from you.

Labs are easily motivated with food in training, but eventually they must be weaned from continuous food rewards.

DID YOU KNOW?

Practice Makes Perfect!

• Have training lessons with your dog every day in several short segments—three to five times a day for a few minutes at a time is ideal.

• Do not have long practice sessions. The dog will become easily bored.

• Never practice when you are tired, ill, worried or in an otherwise negative mood. This will transmit to the dog and may have an adverse effect on its performance.

Think fun, short and above all POSITIVE! End each session on a high note, rather than a failed exercise, and make sure to give a lot of praise. Enjoy the training and help your dog enjoy it, too.

Say 'Sit' and slowly raise your food hand from in front of the dog's nose up over his head so that he is looking at the ceiling. As he bends his head upward, he will have to bend his knees to maintain his balance. As he bends his knees, he will assume a sit position. At that point, release the food treat and praise lavishly with comments such as 'Good dog! Good sit!', etc. Remember to always praise enthusiastically, because dogs relish verbal praise from their owners and feel so proud of themselves whenever they accomplish a behaviour.

You will not use food forever in getting the dog to obey your commands. Food is only used to

Teaching the down is simple if you understand how a dog considers the down position.

teach new behaviours, and once the dog knows what you want when you give a specific command, you will wean him off of the food treats but still maintain the verbal praise. After all, you will always have your voice with you, but there will be many times when you have no food rewards yet you expect the dog to obey.

TEACHING DOWN

Teaching the down exercise is easy when you understand how the dog perceives the down position, and it is very difficult when you do not. In addition, teaching the down exercise using the wrong method can sometimes make the dog develop such a fear of the down that he either runs away when you say 'Down' or he attempts to bite the person who tries to force him down.

Have the dog sit close alongside your left leg, facing in the same direction as you are. Hold the lead in your left hand and a food treat in your right. Now place your left hand lightly on the top of the dog's shoulders where they meet above the spinal cord. Do not push down on the dog's shoulders; simply rest your left hand there so you can guide the dog to lie down close to your left leg rather than to swing away from your side when he drops.

Now place the food hand at the dog's nose, say 'Down' very softly (almost a whisper), and

It is easy to teach a Labrador the sit/stay once he understands the sit command.

slowly lower the food hand to the dog's front feet. When the food hand reaches the floor, begin moving it forward along the floor in front of the dog. Keep talking softly to the dog, saying things like, 'Do you want this treat? You can do this, good dog.' Your reassuring tone of voice will help calm the dog as he tries to follow the food hand in order to get the treat.

When the dog's elbows touch the floor, release the food and praise softly. Try to get the dog to maintain that down position for several seconds before you let him sit up again. The goal here is to get the dog to settle down and not feel threatened in the down position.

the dog, toe to toe, as he licks and nibbles the treat. Be sure to keep his head facing upward to maintain the sit position. Count to five and then swing around to stand next to the dog again with him on your left. As soon as you get back to the original position, release the food and praise lavishly.

To teach the down/stay, do the down as previously described. As soon as the dog lies down, say 'Stay' and step out on your right foot just as you did in the sit/stay. Count to five and then return to stand beside the dog with him on your left side. Release the treat and praise as always.

Within a week or ten days, you can begin to add a bit of distance between you and your dog when you leave him. When you do, use your left hand open with the palm facing the dog as a stay signal, much the same as the hand signal a police officer uses to stop traffic at an intersection. Hold the food treat in your right hand as before, but this time the food is

The stay command is taught in increments. Gradually add distance between you and your dog as you give him the stay command.

90

TEACHING STAY

It is easy to teach the dog to stay in either a sit or a down position. Again, we use food and praise during the teaching process as we help the dog to understand exactly what it is that we are expecting him to do.

To teach the sit/stay, start with the dog sitting on your left side as before and hold the lead in your left hand. Have a food treat in your right hand and place your food hand at the dog's nose. Say 'Stay' and step out on your right foot to stand directly in front of

---

DID YOU KNOW?

A dog in jeopardy never lies down. He stays alert on his feet because instinct tells him that he may have to run away or fight for his survival. Therefore, if a dog feels threatened or anxious, he will not lie down. Consequently, it is important to have the dog calm and relaxed as he learns the down exercise.

not touching the dog's nose. He will watch the food hand and quickly learn that he is going to get that treat as soon as you return to his side.

When you can stand 1 metre away from your dog for 30 seconds, you can then begin building time and distance in both stays. Eventually, the dog can be expected to remain in the stay position for prolonged periods of time until you return to him or call him to you. Always praise lavishly when he stays.

TEACHING COME

If you make teaching 'Come' a fun experience, you should never have a 'student' that does not love the game or that fails to come when called. The secret, it seems, is never to teach the word 'Come.'

At times when an owner most wants his dog to come when called, the owner is likely upset or anxious and he allows these feelings to come through in the tone of his voice when he calls his dog. Hearing that desperation in his owner's voice, the dog fears the results of going to him and therefore either disobeys outright or runs in the opposite direction. The secret, therefore, is to teach the dog a game and, when you want him to come to you, simply play the game. It is practically a no-fail solution!

To begin, have several members of your family take a few food treats and each go into a different room in the house. Take turns calling the dog, and each person should celebrate the dog's finding him with a treat and lots of happy praise. When a person calls the dog, he is actually inviting the dog to find him and get a treat as a reward for 'winning.'

A few turns of the 'Where are you?' game and the dog will figure out that everyone is playing the game and that each person has a big celebration awaiting his success at locating them. Once he learns to love the game, simply calling out 'Where are you?' will bring him running from wherever he is when he hears that all-important question.

The come command is recognised as one of the most important things to teach a dog, so it is interesting to note that

Teaching your Lab to retrieve is building on a natural tendency. Labs LOVE to retrieve.

Teaching the Lab to heel may be a difficult exercise at first. But, if you want to take walks with your dog, it is a necessary training.

Children particularly love to play this game with their dogs. Children can hide in smaller places like a shower or bathtub, behind a bed or under a table. The dog needs to work a little bit harder to find these hiding places, but when he does he loves to celebrate with a treat and a tussle with a favourite youngster.

TEACHING HEEL

Heeling means that the dog walks beside the owner without pulling. It takes time and patience on the owner's part to succeed at teaching the dog that he (the owner) will not proceed unless the dog is walking calmly beside him. Pulling out ahead on the lead is definitely not acceptable.

there are trainers who work with thousands of dogs and never teach the actual word 'Come.' Yet these dogs will race to respond to a person who uses the dog's name followed by 'Where are you?' In one instance, for example, a woman has a 12-year-old companion dog who went blind, but who never fails to locate her owner when asked, 'Where are you?'

Begin with holding the lead in your left hand as the dog sits beside your left leg. Hold the loop end of the lead in your right hand but keep your left hand short on the lead so it keeps the dog in close next to you.

Say 'Heel' and step forward on your left foot. Keep the dog close to you and take three steps. Stop and have the dog sit next to you in what we now call the 'heel position.' Praise verbally, but do not touch the dog. Hesitate a

> **DID YOU KNOW?**
> If you begin teaching the heel by taking long walks and letting the dog pull you along, he misinterprets this action as an acceptable form of taking a walk. When you pull back on the lead to counteract his pulling, he reads that tug as a signal to pull even harder!

moment and begin again with 'Heel,' taking three steps and stopping, at which point the dog is told to sit again.

Your goal here is to have the dog walk those three steps without pulling on the lead. When he will walk calmly beside you for three steps without pulling, increase the number of steps you take to five. When he will walk politely beside you while you take five steps, you can increase the length of your walk to ten steps. Keep increasing the length of your stroll until the dog will walk quietly beside you without pulling as long as you want him to heel. When you stop heeling, indicate to the dog that the exercise is over by verbally praising as you pet him and say 'OK, good dog.' The 'OK' is used as a release word meaning that the exercise is finished and the dog is free to relax.

If you are dealing with a dog who insists on pulling you around, simply 'put on your brakes' and stand your ground until the dog realises that the two of you are not going anywhere until he is beside you and moving at your pace, not his. It may take some time just standing there to convince the dog that you are the leader and you will be the one to decide on the direction and speed of your travel.

Each time the dog looks up at you or slows down to give a slack lead between the two of you, quietly praise him and say, 'Good heel. Good dog.' Eventually, the dog will begin to respond and within a few days he will be walking politely beside you without pulling on the lead. At first, the training sessions should be kept short and very positive; soon the dog will be able to walk nicely with you for increasingly longer distances. Remember also to give the dog free time and the opportunity to run and play when you are done with heel practice.

> **DID YOU KNOW?**
> The puppy should also have regular play and exercise sessions when he is with you or a family member. Exercise for a very young puppy can consist of a short walk around the house or garden. Playing can include fetching games with a large ball or a special raggy. (All puppies teethe and need soft things upon which to chew.) Remember to restrict play periods to indoors within his living area (the family room for example) until he is completely housetrained.

WEANING OFF FOOD IN TRAINING

Food is used in training new behaviours, yet once the dog understands what behaviour goes with a specific command, it is time to start weaning him off the food treats. At first, give a treat after each exercise. Then, start to

Perhaps the most simple training is teaching your Lab to retrieve in the water. Usually he won't be able to wait to jump in.

give a treat only after every other exercise. Mix up the times when you offer a food reward and the times when you only offer praise so that the dog will never know when he is going to receive both food and praise and when he is going to receive only praise. This is called a variable ratio reward system and it proves successful because there is always the chance that the owner will produce a treat, so the dog never stops trying for that reward. No matter what, ALWAYS give verbal praise.

DID YOU KNOW?

Occasionally, a dog and owner who have not attended formal classes have been able to earn entry-level titles by obtaining competition rules and regulations from a local kennel club and practising on their own to a degree of perfection. Obtaining the higher level titles, however, almost always requires extensive training under the tutelage of experienced instructors. In addition, the more difficult levels require more specialised equipment whereas the lower levels do not.

OBEDIENCE CLASSES

As previously discussed, it is a good idea to enrol in an obedience class if one is available in your area. Many areas have dog clubs that offer basic obedience training as well as preparatory classes for obedience competition. There are also local dog trainers who offer similar classes.

At obedience trials, dogs can earn titles at various levels of competition. The beginning levels of competition include basic behaviours such as sit, down, heel, etc. The more advanced levels of competition include jumping, retrieving, scent discrimination and signal work. The advanced levels require a dog and owner to put a lot of time and effort into their training; the titles that can be earned at these levels of competition are very prestigious.

OTHER ACTIVITIES FOR LIFE

Whether a dog is trained in the structured environment of a class or alone with his owner at home, there are many activities that can bring fun and rewards to both owner and dog once they have mastered basic control. The Labrador Retriever is one of the most tractable breeds around, and thus has earned the distinction of frequently being trained for guide dog and service work. This tractability translates into a pet dog who can be trained to do many things with his owner.

Teaching the dog to help out around the home, in the garden or on the farm provides great satisfaction to both dog and owner. In addition, the dog's help makes life a little easier for his owner and raises his stature as a valued companion to his family. It helps give the dog a purpose; it helps to keep his mind occupied and provides an outlet for his energy.

Backpacking is an exciting and healthful activity that the dog can be taught without assistance from more than his owner. The exercise of walking and climbing is good for man and dog alike, and the bond that they develop together is priceless.

Labrador Retrievers have been very successfully used as guide dogs for the blind.

Yellow Labrador being trained for guide dog work at The Seeing Eye®, Morristown, NJ, USA.

If you are interested in participating in organised competition with your Labrador Retriever, there are other activities other than obedience in which you and your dog can become involved. Agility is a popular and fun sport where dogs run through an obstacle course that includes various jumps, tunnels and other exercises to test the dog's speed and coordination. The owners often run through the course beside their dogs to give commands and to guide them through the course. Although competitive, the focus is on fun—it's fun to do and fun to watch, as well as great exercise.

Field trials and gundog trials are also popular with owners of

retriever breeds, since these activities are suited to the dogs' original purpose. These trials evaluate the Labrador's ability as a hunting companion, as they are expected to accompany a hunter and retrieve any type of game.

Labs love sports. Jumping, swimming, running and backpacking are almost natural endeavours for a Lab.

Health Care of Labrador Retrievers

Dogs, being mammals like human beings, suffer many of the same physical illnesses as people. They might even share many of the psychological problems. Since people usually know more about human diseases than canine maladies, many of the terms used in this chapter will be the familiar terms, not necessarily those used by veterinary surgeons. We'll still use the term X-RAY, instead of the more acceptable term RADIOGRAPH. We will also use the familiar term SYMPTOMS even though dogs don't have symptoms, dogs have CLINICAL SIGNS. SYMPTOMS, by the way, are verbal descriptions of the patient's feelings. Since dogs can't speak, we have to look for clinical signs...but we still use the term SYMPTOMS in this book.

As a general rule, medicine is PRACTISED. That term is not arbi-

Your veterinary surgeon will be your dog's friend throughout his life.

trary. Medicine is an art. It is a constant changing art as we learn more and more about genetics, electronic aids (like CAT scans) and opinions. There are many dog maladies, like canine hip dysplasia, which are not universally treated in the same manner. Some veterinary surgeons opt for surgery more often than others.

SELECTING A VETERINARY SURGEON

Your selection of a veterinary surgeon should not be based upon personality (as most are) but upon their convenience to your home. You want a doctor who is close as you might have emergencies or multiple visits for treatments. You want a doctor who has services that you might require such as a tattooing, grooming facilities, who makes sophisticated pet supplies available and who has a

Veterinary surgeon examining an x-ray. You should befriend a vet before you buy your Labrador Retriever puppy.

good reputation for ability and responsiveness. There is nothing more frustrating than having to wait a day or more to get a response from a veterinary surgeon.

All veterinary surgeons are licensed and their diplomas and/or certificates should be displayed in their waiting rooms. There are, however, many veterinary specialties which usually require further studies and internships. There are specialists in heart problems (veterinary cardiologists), skin problems (veterinary dermatologists), teeth and gum problems (veterinary dentists), eye problems (veterinary ophthalmologists), X-rays (veterinary radiologists), and surgeons who have specialties in bones, muscles or other organs. Most veterinary surgeons do routine surgery such as

neutering, stitching up wounds and docking tails for those breeds in which such is required for show purposes. When the problem affecting your dog is serious, it is not unusual or impudent to get another medical opinion. You might also want to compare costs between several veterinary surgeons. Sophisticated health care and veterinary services can be very costly. Don't be bashful to discuss these costs with your veterinary surgeon or his (her) staff. It is not infrequent that important decisions are based upon financial considerations.

PREVENTATIVE MEDICINE
It is much easier, less costly and more effective to practise preventative medicine than to fight bouts of illness and disease.

All veterinary surgeons are licensed and all have been taught to read x-rays, but there are specialists called veterinary radiologists who are consulted for the fine details of x-ray interpretation.

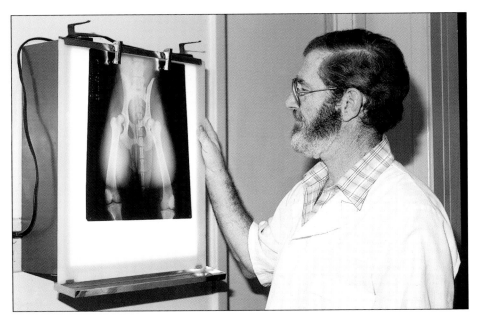

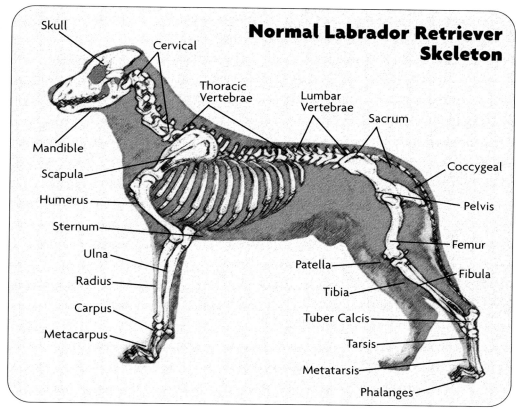

Normal Labrador Retriever Skeleton

Skull, Cervical, Thoracic Vertebrae, Lumbar Vertebrae, Sacrum, Coccygeal, Mandible, Scapula, Humerus, Sternum, Ulna, Radius, Carpus, Metacarpus, Patella, Tibia, Tuber Calcis, Tarsis, Metatarsis, Phalanges, Pelvis, Femur, Fibula

Properly bred puppies come from parents that were selected based upon their genetic disease profile. Their mothers should have been vaccinated, free of all internal and external parasites, and properly nourished. For these reasons, a visit to the veterinary surgeon who cared for the dam (mother) is recommended. The dam can pass on disease resistance to her puppies. This resistance can last for 8-10 weeks. She can also pass on parasites and many infections. That's why you should visit the veterinary surgeon who cared for the dam.

WEANING TO FIVE MONTHS OLD
Puppies should be weaned by the time they are about two months old. A puppy that remains for at least eight weeks with its mother and litter mates usually adapts better to other dogs and people later in its life.

In every case, you should have your newly acquired puppy examined by a veterinary surgeon immediately. Vaccination programmes usually begin when the puppy is very young.

The puppy will have its teeth examined, have its skeletal conformation checked, and have its general health checked prior to certification by the veterinary surgeon. Many puppies have problems with their knee caps, eye cataracts and other eye problems, heart murmurs and undescended testicles. They may also have personality problems and your veterinary surgeon might have training in temperament evaluation. More puppies (dogs) are put to sleep because they behave poorly than all other medical conditions combined.

VACCINATION SCHEDULING

Most vaccinations are given by injection and should only be done by a veterinary surgeon. Both he and you should keep a record of the date of the injection, the identification of the vaccine and the amount given. The vaccination scheduling is based on a 15-day cycle. The first vaccinations should start when the puppy is 6-8 weeks old, then 15 days later when it is 10-12 weeks of age and later when it is 14-16 weeks of age. Vaccinations should NEVER be given without a 15-day lapse between injections. Most vaccinations immunise your puppy against viruses.

DID YOU KNOW?

Ridding your puppy of worms is VERY IMPORTANT because certain worms that puppies carry can infect humans, such as tapeworms, hookworms and roundworms.

Since puppies are never housebroken at two to three weeks of age, it is easy for them to pass on the parasites (worms) to humans.

Breeders initiate a deworming programme two weeks after weaning. The routine is repeated every two or three weeks until the puppy is three months old. The breeder from whom you obtained your Labrador Retriever puppy should provide you with the complete details of the deworming programme.

Your veterinary surgeon can prescribe and monitor the programme of deworming for you. The usual programme is treating the puppy every 15-20 days until the puppy is positively worm free.

It is not advised that you treat your puppy with drugs which are not recommended professionally.

Vaccinations are extremely important as infectious diseases can easily be passed from dog to dog.

The usual vaccines contain immunising doses of several different viruses such as distemper, parvovirus, parainfluenza and hepatitis. There are other vaccines available when the puppy is at risk. You should rely upon professional advice. This is especially true for the booster shot programme. Most vaccination programmes require a booster

HEALTH AND VACCINATION SCHEDULE

AGE IN WEEKS:	3RD	6TH	8TH	10TH	12TH	14TH	16TH	20-24TH
Worm Control	✔	✔	✔	✔	✔	✔	✔	✔
Neutering								✔
Heartworm*		✔						✔
Parvovirus		✔		✔		✔		✔
Distemper			✔		✔		✔	
Hepatitis			✔		✔		✔	
Leptospirosis		✔		✔		✔		
Parainfluenza		✔		✔		✔		
Dental Examination			✔					✔
Complete Physical			✔					✔
Temperament Testing			✔					
Coronavirus					✔			
Kennel Cough		✔						
Hip Dysplasia							✔	
Rabies*								✔

Vaccinations are not instantly effective. It takes about two weeks for the dog's immunisation system to develop antibodies. Most vaccinations require annual booster shots. Your veterinary surgeon should guide you in this regard.
*Not applicable in the United Kingdom

when the puppy is a year old, and once a year thereafter. In some cases, circumstances may require more frequent immunisations.

Kennel cough, more formally known as *tracheobronchitis*, is treated with a vaccine which is sprayed into the dog's nostrils.

The effectiveness of a parvovirus vaccination programme can be tested to be certain that the vaccinations are protective. Your veterinary surgeon will explain and manage all of these details.

FIVE MONTHS TO ONE YEAR OF AGE
By the time your puppy is five months old, he should have completed his vaccination programme. During

DID YOU KNOW?
Caring for the puppy starts before the puppy is born by keeping the dam healthy and well-nourished. When the puppy is about three weeks old, it must start its disease-control regimen. The first treatments will be for worms. Most puppies have worms, even if they are tested negative for worms. The test essentially is checking the stool specimens for the eggs of the worms. The worms continually shed eggs except during their dormant stage when they just rest in the tissues of the puppy. During this stage they don't shed eggs and are not evident during a routine examination.

his physical examination he should be evaluated for the common hip dysplasia plus other diseases of the joints. There are tests to assist in the prediction of these problems. Other tests can also be run, such as the parvovirus antibody titer, which can

Genetic predisposition to hip dysplasia and skin problems can easily be passed from mother to puppy.

assess the effectiveness of the vaccination programme.

Unless you intend to breed or show your dog, neutering the puppy at six months of age is recommended. Discuss this with your veterinary surgeon.

By the time your Labrador Retriever is seven or eight months of age, he can be seriously evaluated for his conformation to the club standard, thus determining his show potential and his desirability as a sire or dam. If the puppy is not top class and therefore is not a candidate for a serious breeding programme, most professionals advise neutering the puppy. Neutering has proven to be extremely beneficial to both male and female puppies. Besides the obvious impossibility of pregnancy, it inhibits (but does not prevent) breast cancer in bitches and prostate cancer in male dogs.

Blood tests are performed for heartworm infestation and it is possible

DID YOU KNOW?

As Labrador Retriever puppies become more and more expensive, especially those puppies of high quality for showing and/or breeding, they have a greater chance of being stolen. The usual collar dog tag is, of course, easily removed. But there are two techniques which are becoming widely utilised for identification.

The puppy microchip implantation involves the injection of a small microchip, about the size of a corn kernel, under the skin of the dog. If your dog shows up at a clinic or shelter, or is offered for resale under less than savory circumstances, it can be positively identified by the microchip. The microchip is scanned and a registry quickly identifies you as the owner. This is not only protection against theft, but should the dog run away or go chasing a varmint and get lost, you have a fair chance of getting it back.

Tattooing is done on various parts of the dog, from its belly to its cheeks. The number tattooed can be your telephone number or any other number which you can easily memorise. When professional dog thieves see a tattooed dog, they usually lose interest in it. Both microchipping and tattooing can be done at your local veterinary clinic. For the safety of our Labrador Retrievers, no laboratory facility or dog broker will accept a tattooed dog as stock.

that your puppy will be placed on a preventative therapy which will prevent heartworm infection as well as control other internal parasites.

DID YOU KNOW?

A dental examination is in order when the dog is between six months and one year of age and any permanent teeth that have erupted incorrectly can be corrected. It is important to begin a brushing regimen, preferably using a two-sided brushing technique, whereby both sides of the tooth are brushed at the same time. Durable nylon and safe edible chews should be a part of your puppy's arsenal for good health, good teeth and pleasant breath. The vast majority of dogs three to four years old and older has diseases of their gums from lack of dental attention. Using the various types of dental chews can be very effective in controlling dental plaque.

By the time your dog is a year old, you should have become very comfortable with your local veterinary surgeon and have agreed on scheduled visits for booster vaccinations. Blood tests should now be taken regularly, for comparative purposes, for such variables as cholesterol and triglyceride levels, thyroid hormones, liver enzymes, blood cell counts, etc.

The eyes, ears, nose and throat should be examined regularly and annual cleaning of the teeth is a ritual. For teeth scaling, the dog must be anaesthetised.

DOGS OLDER THAN ONE YEAR

Continue to visit the veterinary surgeon at least once a year. There is no such disease as *old age*, but bodily functions do change with age, and the eyes and ears are no longer as efficient. Neither are the internal workings of the liver, kidneys and intestines. Proper dietary changes, recommended by your veterinary surgeon, can make life more pleasant for the ageing Labrador Retriever and you.

SKIN PROBLEMS IN LABRADOR RETRIEVERS

Veterinary surgeons are consulted by dog owners for skin problems more than any other group of diseases or maladies. Dogs' skin is almost as sensitive as human skin and both suffer almost the same maladies. (Though the occurrence of acne in dogs is rare!) For this reason, veterinary dermatology has developed into a specialty practised by many veterinary surgeons.

Since many skin problems have visual symptoms which are almost identical, it requires the skill of an experienced veterinary dermatologist to identify and cure many of the more severe skin disorders. Simply put, if your dog is suffering from a

You can always tell which puppy is going to be the dominant one, can't you?

103

skin disorder, seek professional assistance as quickly as possible. As with all diseases, the earlier a problem is identified and treated, the more successful is the cure.

Pet shops sell many treatments for skin problems. Most of the treatments are simply directed at symptoms and not the underlying problem(s).

Inherited Skin Problems

Many skin disorders are inherited and some are fatal. Acrodermatitis is an inherited disease which is transmitted by BOTH parents. The

DID YOU KNOW?

There is a 1:4 chance of a puppy getting this fatal gene combination from two parents with recessive genes for acrodermatitis:

AA= NORMAL, HEALTHY
aa= FATAL
Aa= RECESSIVE, NORMAL APPEARING

If the female parent has an Aa gene and the male parent has an Aa gene, the chances are one in four that the puppy will have the fatal genetic combination aa.

Dam

Sire	A	a	♀
A	AA	Aa	
a	Aa	aa	
♂			

DO YOU KNOW ABOUT HIP DYSPLASIA?

Hip dysplasia is a fairly common condition found in Labrador Retrievers, as well as other breeds. When a dog has hip dysplasia, its hind leg has an incorrectly formed hip joint. By constant use of the hip joint, it becomes more and more loose, wears abnormally and may become arthritic.

Hip dysplasia can only be confirmed with an X-ray, but certain symptoms may indicate a problem. Your Labrador Retriever may have a hip dysplasia problem if it walks in a peculiar manner, hops instead of smoothly running, uses his hinds legs in unison (to keep the pressure off the weak joint), has trouble getting up from a prone position and always sits with both legs together on one side of its body.

As the dog matures, it may adapt well to life with a bad hip, but in a few years the arthritis develops and many Labrador Retrievers with hip dysplasia become cripples.

Hip dysplasia is considered an inherited disease and can usually be diagnosed when the dog is three to nine months old. Some experts claim that a special diet might help your puppy outgrow the bad hip, but the usual treatments are surgical: the removal of the pectineus muscle, the removal of the round part of the femur, reconstructing the pelvis and replacing the hip with an artificial one. All of these surgical interventions are expensive, but they are usually very successful. Follow the advice of your veterinary surgeon.

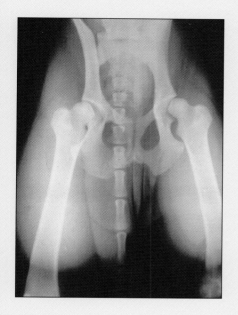

Compare the two hip joints and you'll understand dysplasia. Hip dysplasia is a badly worn hip joint caused by improper fit of the bone into the socket. It is easily the most common hip problem in Labrador Retrievers.

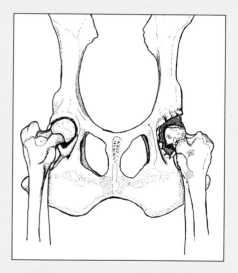

The healthy hip joint on the left and the unhealthy hip joint on the right.

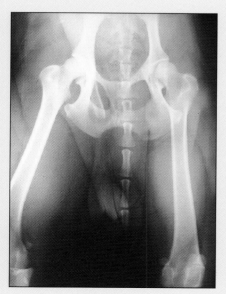

Hip dysplasia can only be positively diagnosed by X-ray. Labrador Retrievers manifest the problem when they are between four and nine months of age, the so-called fast-growth period.

parents, which appear (phenotypically) normal, have a recessive gene for acrodermatitis, meaning that they carry, but are not affected by, the disease.

Dogs can be allergic to their food.

Acrodermatitis is just one example of how difficult it is to diagnose and treat many dog diseases. The cost and skills required to ascertain whether two dogs should be mated is too high even though puppies with acrodermatitis rarely reach two years of age.

Other inherited skin problems are usually not as fatal as acrodermatitis. All inherited diseases must be diagnosed and treated by a veterinary

specialist. There are active programmes being undertaken by many veterinary pharmaceutical manufacturers to solve most, if not all, of the common skin problems of dogs.

PARASITE BITES
Many of us are allergic to mosquito bites. The bites itch, erupt and may even become infected. Dogs have the same reaction to fleas, ticks and/or mites. When you feel the prick of the mosquito when it bites you, you have a chance to kill it with your hand. Unfortunately, when your dog is bitten by a flea, tick or mite, it can only scratch it away or bite it. By the time the dog has been bitten, the parasite has done some of its damage. It may also have laid eggs to cause further problems in the near future. The itching from parasite bites is probably due to the saliva injected into the site when the parasite sucks the dog's blood.

AIRBORNE ALLERGIES
Another interesting allergy is pollen allergy. Humans have hay fever, rose fever and other fevers with which they suffer during the pollinating season. Many dogs suffer the same allergies. So when the pollen count

Your Labrador Retriever's skin and coat should be checked often for any sign of irritation, especially after he has been outdoors.

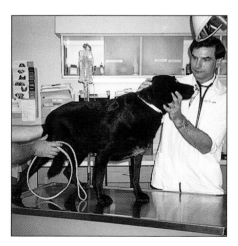

> **DID YOU KNOW?**
> Chances are that you and your dog will have the same allergies. Your allergies are readily recognisable and usually easily treated. Your dog's allergies may be masked.

is high, your dog might suffer. Don't expect them to sneeze and have runny noses like humans. Dogs react to pollen allergies the same way they react to fleas—they scratch and bite themselves. Labrador Retrievers are very susceptible to airborne pollen allergies.

Dogs, like humans, can be tested for allergens. Discuss the testing with your veterinary dermatologist.

FOOD ALLERGIES

Dogs are allergic to many foods which are best-sellers and highly recommended by breeders and veterinary surgeons. Changing the brand of food that you buy may not eliminate the problem because the element of the food to which the dog is allergic may also be contained in the new brand.

Recognising a food allergy is difficult. Humans vomit or have rashes when they eat a food to which they are allergic. Dogs neither vomit nor

Disease	What is it?	What causes it?	Symptoms
Leptospirosis	Severe disease that affects the internal organs; can be spread to people.	A bacterium, which is often carried by rodents, that enters through mucous membranes and spreads quickly throughout the body.	Range from fever, vomiting and loss of appetite in less severe cases to shock, irreversible kidney damage and possibly death in most severe cases.
Rabies	Potentially deadly virus that infects warm-blooded mammals. Not seen in United Kingdom.	Bite from a carrier of the virus, mainly wild animals.	1st stage: dog exhibits change in behaviour, fear. 2nd stage: dog's behaviour becomes more aggressive. 3rd stage: loss of coordination, trouble with bodily functions.
Parvovirus	Highly contagious virus, potentially deadly.	Ingestion of the virus, which is usually spread through the faeces of infected dogs.	Most common: severe diarrhoea. Also vomiting, fatigue, lack of appetite.
Kennel cough	Contagious respiratory infection.	Combination of types of bacteria and virus. Most common: *Bordetella bronchiseptica* bacteria and parainfluenza virus.	Chronic cough.
Distemper	Disease primarily affecting respiratory and nervous system.	Virus that is related to the human measles virus.	Mild symptoms such as fever, lack of appetite and mucous secretion progress to evidence of brain damage, 'hard pad.'
Hepatitis	Virus primarily affecting the liver.	Canine adenovirus type I (CAV-1). Enters system when dog breathes in particles.	Lesser symptoms include listlessness, diarrhoea, vomiting. More severe symptoms include 'blue-eye' (clumps of virus in eye).
Coronavirus	Virus resulting in digestive problems.	Virus is spread through infected dog's faeces.	Stomach upset evidenced by lack of appetite, vomiting, diarrhoea.

(usually) develop a rash. Instead they itch, scratch and bite, thus making the diagnosis extremely difficult. While pollen allergies and parasite bites are usually seasonal, food allergies are year-round problems.

TREATING FOOD PROBLEMS
Handling food allergies and food intolerance yourself is possible. Put your dog on a diet which it has never had. Obviously if it never ate this new food it can't have been allergic or intolerant of it. Start with a single ingredient which is NOT in the dog's diet at the present time. Ingredients like chopped beef or fish are common in dog's diets, so try something more exotic like rabbit, pheasant or even just vegetables such as potatoes. Keep the dog on this diet (with no additives) for a month. If the symptoms of food allergy or intolerance disappear, chances are that you have defined the cause.

Don't think that the single ingredient cured the problem. You still must find a suitable diet and ascertain which ingredient in the old diet was objectionable. This is most easily done by adding ingredients to the new diet one at a time until the problem is solved. Let the dog stay on the modified diet for a month before you add another ingredient.

An alternative method is to carefully study the ingredients in the diet to which your dog is allergic or intolerant. Identify the main ingredient in this diet and eliminate the main ingredient by buying a different food which does not have that

A scanning electron micrograph (S. E. M.) of a dog flea, Ctenocephalides canis.

ingredient. Keep experimenting until the symptoms disappear after one month on the new diet.

EXTERNAL PARASITES
Of all the problems to which dogs are prone, none is more well known and frustrating than fleas. *Fleas,* which usually refers to fleas, ticks and mites, are relatively simple to cure but difficult to prevent. The opposite is true for the parasites which are harboured inside the body. They are a bit more difficult to cure but they are easier to control.

FLEAS
It is possible to control flea infestation but you have to understand the life cycle of a typical flea in order to control them. Basically fleas are a summertime problem and their effective treatment (destruction) is environmental. The problem is that there is no single flea control medicine (insecticide) which can be used in every flea infested area. To understand flea control you must apply suitable treatment to the weak link in the life cycle of the flea.

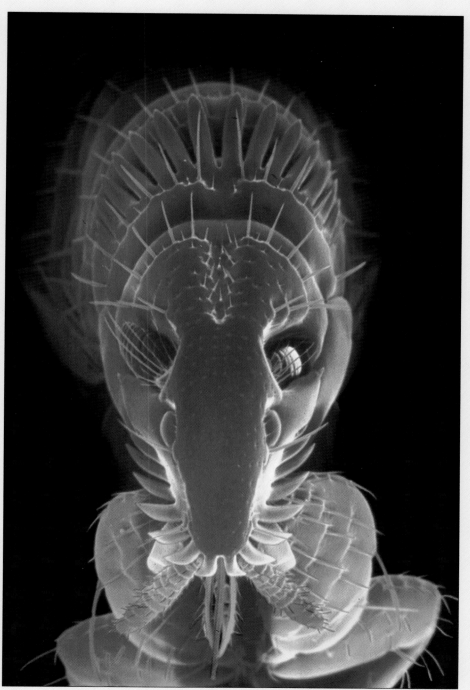

A scanning electron micrograph of a dog or cat flea, Ctenocephalides magnified more than 100X. This has been coloured for effect.

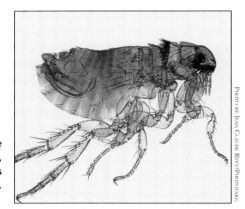

A male dog flea, Ctenocephalides canis.

Photo by Jean Claude Revy/Phototake.

DID YOU KNOW?

Average size dogs, like Labrador Retrievers, can pass 1,360,000 roundworm eggs every day.

With an average of 1 million Labrador Retrievers in the world, the world is saturated with 1,300 metric tonnes of dog faeces.

These faeces contain 15,000,000,000 roundworm eggs.

7-31% of home gardens and children's play boxes in the U. S. contained roundworm eggs.

Flushing dog's faeces down the toilet is not a safe practice because the usual sewage treatments do not destroy roundworm eggs.

Infected Labrador Retriever puppies start shedding roundworm eggs at 3 weeks of age. They can be infected by their mother's milk.

THE LIFE CYCLE OF A FLEA

Fleas are found in four forms: eggs, larvae, pupae and adults. You really need a low-power microscope or hand lens to identify a living flea's eggs, pupae or larva. They spend their whole lives on your Labrador Retriever unless they are forcibly removed by brushing, bathing, scratching or biting.

Several species infest both dog and cats. The dog flea is scientifically known as *Ctenocephalides*

The eggs of the dog flea.

Male cat fleas, Ctenocephalides felis, are very commonly found on dogs.

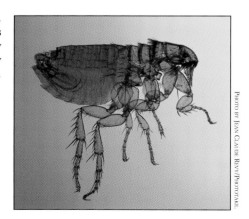

Photo by Jean Claude Revy/Phototake.

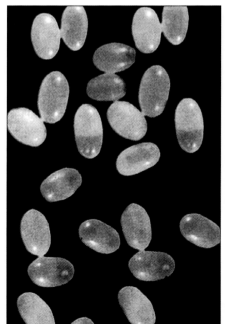

The Life Cycle of the Flea

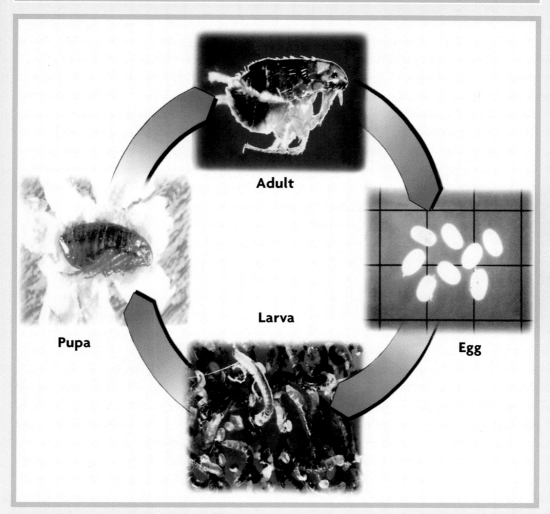

Adult

Pupa

Larva

Egg

The Life Cycle of the Flea was posterised by Fleabusters. Poster courtesy of Fleabusters®, Rx for Fleas.

Dwight R. Kuhn's magnificent action photo showing a flea jumping from a dog's back.

PHOTO BY DWIGHT R. KUHN

canis while the cat flea is *Cteno-cephalides felis*. Cat fleas are very common on dogs.

Fleas lay eggs while they are in residence on your dog. These eggs

Dogs pick up fleas outdoors, too.

Magnified head of a dog flea, Ctenocephalides canis.

do not adhere to the hair of your dog and they simply fall off almost as soon as they dry (they may be a bit damp when initially laid). These eggs are the reservoir of future flea infestations. If your dog scratches himself and is able to dislodge a few fleas, they simply fall off and

await a future chance to attack a dog...or even a person. *Yes, fleas from dogs bite people.* That's why it is so important to control fleas both on the dog and in the dog's entire environment. You must, therefore, treat the dog and the environment simultaneously.

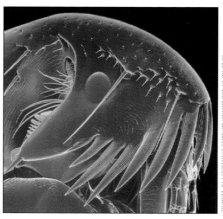

S. E. M. BY DR. DENNIS KUNKEL, UNIVERSITY OF HAWAII

Photo by Dwight R. Kuhn

DE-FLEAING THE HOME

Cleanliness is the simple rule. If you have a cat living with your dog, the matter is more complicated since most dog fleas are actually cat fleas. But since cats climb onto many areas that are never accessible to dogs (like window sills, table tops, etc.), you have to clean all of these areas, too. The hard floor surfaces (tiles, wood, stone and linoleum) must be mopped several times a day. Drops of food onto the floor are actually food for flea larvae! All rugs and furniture must be vacuumed several times a day. Don't forget closets, under furniture, cushions. A study has reported that a vacuum cleaner with a beater bar can only remove 20% of the larvae and 50% of the eggs. The vacuum bags should be discarded into a sealed plastic bag or burned. The vacuum machine itself should be cleaned. The outdoor area to which your dog has access must also be treated with an insecticide.

This all sounds like a lot of work! It is and, therefore, you should choose a top-quality insecticide and apply it correctly.

While there are many drugs available to kill fleas on the dog itself, such as the miracle drug ivermectin, it is best to have the de-fleaing and de-worming supervised by your vet. Ivermectin is effective against many external and internal parasites including heartworms, roundworms, tapeworms, flukes, ticks and mites. It has not been approved for use to control these pests, but veterinary surgeons frequently use it anyway.

Human lice look like dog lice; the two are closely related.

De-fleaing your dog is easy, it's ridding the surrounding environment of fleas that is difficult.

STERILISING THE ENVIRONMENT

Besides cleaning your home with vacuum cleaners and mops, you have to treat the outdoor range of your dog. This means trimming bushes, spreading insecticide and being careful not to poison areas in which fishes or other animals reside.

The dog tick, Dermacentor variabilis, is probably the most common tick found on dogs. Look at the strength in its eight legs! No wonder it's hard to detach them.

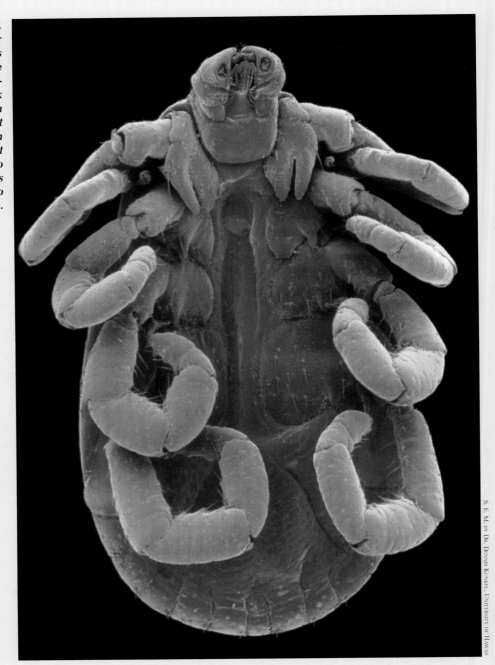

This is best done by an outside service specialising in de-fleaing. Your vet should be able to recommend a local service.

TICKS AND MITES

Though not as common as fleas, ticks and mites are found all over the tropical and temperate world. They don't bite, like fleas, rather they harpoon. They dig their sharp

The head of the dog tick, Dermacentor variabilis.

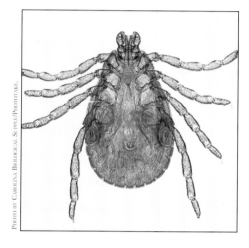

A brown dog tick, Rhipicephalus sanguineus, *is an uncommon but annoying tick found on dogs.*

The dog tick *Dermacentor variabilis* may well be the most common dog tick in many geographical areas, especially those areas where the climate is hot and humid.

Most dog ticks have life expectancies of a week to six months, depending upon climatic conditions. They can neither jump

proboscis (nose) into the dog's skin and drink the blood. Their only food and drink is dog's blood. Dogs can get Lyme disease, Rocky Mountain spotted fever (normally found in the U.S.A. only), paralysis and many other maladies, from ticks and mites. They may live where fleas are found except they like to hide in cracks or seams in walls wherever dogs live. They are controlled the same way fleas are controlled.

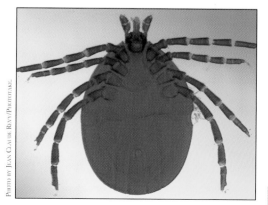

The dog tick of the genus Ixode.

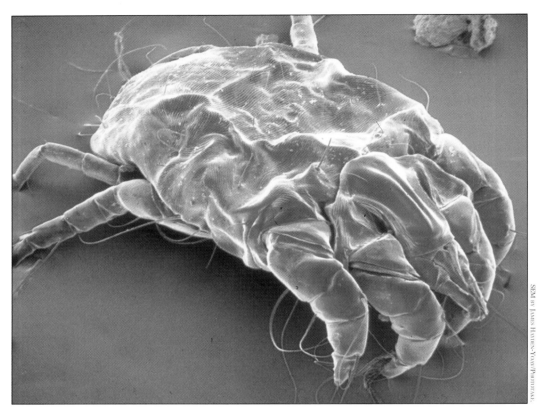

SEM by James Hayden-Yoav/Phototake

Magnified view of the mange mite, Psoroptes bovis.

nor fly, but they can crawl slowly and can range up to 5 metres (16 feet) to reach a sleeping or unsuspecting dog.

MANGE

Mites cause a skin irritation called *mange.* Some are contagious, like *Cheyletiella, ear mites, scabies and chiggers.* The non-contagious mites are Demodex. The most serious of the mites is the ear mite infestation. Ear mites are usually controlled with ivermectin.

It is essential that your dog be treated for mange as quickly as possi-ble because some forms of mange are transmissible to people.

AUTO-IMMUNE SKIN CONDITIONS

Auto-immune skin conditions are commonly referred to as being aller-gic to yourself. Allergies, though, usually result in inflammatory reac-tions to an outside stimulus. Auto-immune diseases cause serious dam-age to the tissues which are involved.

The best known auto-immune dis-ease is lupus. It affects people as well as dogs. The symptoms are very variable and may affect the kidneys, bones, blood chemistry and skin. It can be fatal to both dogs and humans, though it is not thought to be transmissible. It is usually successfully treated with cortisone, prednisone or similar corticosteroid, but extensive use of these drugs can have harmful side effects.

ACRAL LICK GRANULOMA

Labrador Retrievers and other dogs about the same size (like German Shepherd Dogs), have a very poorly understood syndrome called *acral lick*. The manifestation of the problem is the dog's tireless attack at a specific area of the body, almost always the legs. They lick so intensively that they remove the hair and skin leaving an ugly, large wound. There is no absolute cure, but corticosteroids are the most common treatment.

SIMULATED MEDICAL CONDITION FOR EDUCATIONAL PURPOSES ONLY.

INTERNAL PARASITES

Most animals—fishes, birds and mammals, including dogs and humans—have worms and other parasites which

Acral lick syndrome results in a large open wound, a lick granuloma, usually on the dog's leg.

S.E.M. BY JAMES HAYDEN-YOAV/PHOTOTAKE.

The dog mange mite is frequently seen on cows as well.

117

DEFENSE AGAINST FLEAS

• Add a small amount of pennyroyal or eucalyptus oil to your dog's bath. These natural remedies repel fleas.
• Supplement your dog's food with fresh garlic (minced or grated) and a hearty amount of brewer's yeast, both of which ward off fleas.
• Use a flea comb on your dog daily. Submerge fleas in a cup of bleach to kill them.
• Confine the dog to only a few rooms to limit the spread of fleas in the home.
• Vacuum daily...and get all of the crevices!
• Cover cushions where your dog sleeps with towels. Wash the towels—along with your dog's regular bedding—often.
 • Throw away your dog's flea collars. They are a waste of money and do not work!

live inside their bodies. According to Dr Herbert R Axelrod, the fish pathologist, there are two kinds of parasites: dumb and smart. The smart parasites live in peaceful cooperation with their hosts (symbiosis), while the dumb parasites kill their host. Most of the worm infections are relatively easy to control. If they are not controlled they eventually weaken the host dog to the point that other medical problems occur, but they are not dumb parasites.

ROUNDWORMS

The roundworms that infect dogs are scientifically known as *Toxocara canis*. They live in the dog's intestine. The worms shed eggs continually. It

The round-worm can infect both dogs and humans.

PHOTO BY CAROLINA BIOLOGICAL SUPPLY/PHOTOTAKE.

has been estimated that a Labrador Retriever produces about 150 grammes of faeces every day. Each gramme of faeces averages 10,000-12,000 eggs of roundworms. There are no known areas in which dogs roam that do not contain the eggs of roundworms. The greatest danger of roundworms is that they infect people, too! It is wise to have your dog tested regularly for roundworms.

Pigs also have roundworm infections which can be passed to humans and dogs. The typical roundworm parasite is called *Ascaris lumbricoides.*

HOOKWORMS

The worm *Ancylostoma caninum* is commonly called the dog hookworm. It is dangerous to humans and cats. It also has teeth by which it attaches itself to the intestines of the dog. Because it changes the site of its attachment about six times a day, the dog loses blood from each detachment,

DID YOU KNOW?
Humans, rats, squirrels, foxes, coyotes, wolves, mixed breeds of dogs and purebred dogs are all susceptible to tapeworm infection. Except for humans, tapeworms are usually not a fatal infection.

Infected individuals can harbour a thousand parasitic worms.

Tapeworms have two sexes—male and female (many other worms have only one sex—male and female in the same worm).

If dogs eat infected rats or mice, they get the tapeworm disease.

One month after attaching to a dog's intestine, the worm starts shedding eggs. These eggs are infective immediately.

Infective eggs can live for a few months without a host animal.

Roundworms, hookworms, whipworms and tapeworms are just a few of the commonly known worms which infect dogs.

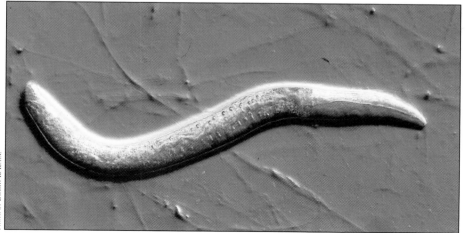

The roundworm, Ascaris lumbricoides, *is found in dogs, pigs and humans.*

119

The roundworm Rhabditis.

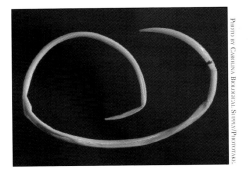

PHOTO BY CAROLINA BIOLOGICAL SUPPLY/PHOTOTAKE.

Male and female hookworms, Ancylostoma caninum, found in Labrador Retrievers.

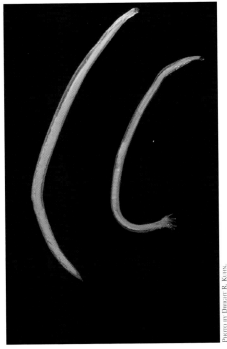

PHOTO BY DWIGHT R. KUHN.

DID YOU KNOW?

Ivermectin is quickly becoming the drug of choice for treating many parasitic skin diseases in dogs.

For some unknown reason, herding German Shepherds, Collies, Old English Sheepdogs, Australian Shepherds, etc., are extremely sensitive to ivermectin.

Ivermectin injections have killed some dogs, but dogs heavily infected with skin disorders may be treated anyway.

The ivermectin reaction is a toxicosis which causes tremors, loss of power to move their muscles, prolonged dilitation of the pupil of the eye, coma (unconsciousness), or cessation of breathing (death).

The toxicosis usually starts from 4-6 hours after ingestion (not injection), or as late as 12 hours. The longer it takes to set in, the milder is the reaction.

Ivermectin should only be prescribed and administered by a vet.

Some ivermectin treatments require two doses.

possibly causing iron-deficiency anaemia. They are easily purged from the dog with many medications, the best of which seems to be ivermectin even though it has not been approved for such use.

TAPEWORMS

There are many species of tapeworms. They are carried by fleas! The dog eats the flea and thus starts the tapeworm cycle. Humans can also be infected with tapeworms, so don't eat fleas! Fleas are so small that your dog could pass them onto your hands, your plate or your food and thus make it possible for you to ingest a flea which is carrying tapeworm eggs.

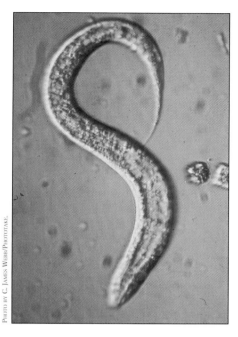

PHOTO BY C. JAMES WEBB/PHOTOTAKE.

PHOTO BY CAROLINA BIOLOGICAL SUPPLY/PHOTOTAKE.

While tapeworm infection is not life threatening in dogs (smart parasite!), it can be the cause of a very serious liver disease for humans. About 50 percent of the humans infected with *Echinococcus multilocularis*, causing alveolar hydatis, perish.

HEARTWORMS

Heartworms are thin, extended worms up to 30 cm (12 in.) long which live in

The infective stage of the hookworm larva.

The head and rostellum (the round prominence on the scolex) of a tapeworm, which infects dogs and humans.

DID YOU KNOW?

Two types of products should be used when treating fleas—a product to treat the pet and a product to treat the home. Adult fleas represent less than 1% of the flea population. The pre-adult fleas (eggs, larvae and pupae) represent more than 99% of the flea population and are found in the environment; it is in the case of pre-adult fleas that products containing an Insect Growth Regulator (IGR) should be used in the home. IGRs are a new class of compounds used to prevent the development of insects. They do not kill the insect outright, but instead use the insect's biology against it to stop it from completing its growth. Products that contain methoprene are the world's first and leading IGRs. Used to control fleas and other insects, this type of IGR will stop flea larvae from developing and protect the house for up to seven months.

121

The heart of a dog infected with canine heartworm, Dirofilaria immitis.

PHOTO BY JAMES E. HAYDEN, RPB/PHOTOTAKE.

DID YOU KNOW?

It was announced in April 1999 that the severe quarantine laws imposed on animals entering Britain from other rabies-free countries would become a thing of the past by April 2001. Rather than being confined to a kennel for six months upon arrival in Britain, animals undergo a series of blood tests and vaccinations, and are identifed by microchip implantation. Qualified pets receive a 'health passport' that allows their owners to travel with them in between Britain and other (mostly European) countries in which rabies does not exist.

Animals from countries such as the United States and Canada, where rabies is a problem, still will be subject to quarantine because a recent infection may not show up in a blood test.

a dog's heart and major blood vessels around the heart. Labrador Retrievers may have up to 200 of these worms. The symptoms may be loss of energy, loss of appetite, coughing, the development of a pot belly and anaemia.

Heartworms are transmitted by mosquitoes. The mosquito drinks the blood of an infected dog and takes in larvae with the blood. The larvae, called microfilaria, develop within the body of the mosquito and are passed on to the next dog bitten after the larvae mature. It takes two to three weeks for the larvae to develop to the infective stage within the body of the mosquito. Dogs should be treated at about six weeks of age, then every six months.

Blood testing for heartworms is not necessarily indicative of how seriously your dog is infected. This is a dangerous disease. Dogs in the United Kingdom are not affected by heartworm.

MEDICAL PROBLEMS MOST FREQUENTLY SEEN IN LABRADOR RETRIEVERS

Condition	Age Affected	Cause	Area Affected
Acral Lick Dermatitis	Any age, males	Unknown	Legs
Cataracts	Less than 1 year	Congenital	Eye
Elbow Dysplasia	4 to 7 mos.	Congenital	Elbow joint
Epilepsy	6 mos. to 3 years	Congenital	Nervous system
Gastric Dilatation (Bloat)	Older dogs	Swallowing air	Stomach
Hip Dysplasia	4 to 9 mos.	Congenital	Hip joint
Hypertrophic Osteodystrophy	3 to 4 mos.	Organism or vitamin imbalance	Bones
Hypothyroidism	1 to 3 years	Lymphocytic thyroiditis	Endocrine system
Liver Disease	Young adulthood	Congenital	Liver
Myopathy	Adults	Congenital	Muscles
Narcolepsy	1 to 5 mos.	Congenital	Sleep Disorder
Osteochondrosis	4 to 7 mos.	Congenital	Cartilage (fore or hinds)
Progressive Retinal Atrophy	Older dogs	Congenital	Retina
Von Willebrand's Disease	Birth	Congenital	Blood

HEALTH OF THE LABRADOR RETRIEVER

By and large, the Labrador Retriever is a healthy dog, blessed with a great enthusiasm for life, inclined toward activity and fresh air. While most Labradors love a romp through the meadow, beach-front or park with their owners, some Labradors tend to be sedentary, especially in their later years. Keeping the Labrador fit and trim is akin to keeping him healthy. Obesity can be a problem in any dog, purebred or mongrel, just as it can be a problem with many humans. Since obesity can compromise the quality of your Labrador's life and shorten his years, it must be considered a serious threat. Studies show that obesity is the most prevalent nutrition-related problems of our pets, and among dogs Labradors tip the scale! Veterinarians and nutrition specialists confirm that this disease has significant ties to lifestyle of the owners. Over-weight owners, inclined to snack and share, have overweight dogs. Labradors by definition are chow hounds, and nothing delights a Labrador more than chomping his way through a bag of crisps! Don't judge your Labrador's happiness by his waist size: he'll be happier if he's trim and active, and he'll be around longer too.

The Labrador Retriever, like most other breeds of purebred dogs, is disposed to a number of genetic diseases. Many veterinary surgeons state that purebred dogs are much more inclined to heredi-tary disorders than are their mixed-breed counterparts.

Epilepsy (described as 'idio-pathic' or of unknown cause) runs in lines of the Labrador, so only certain families are disposed. As in humans, epilepsy is charac-terised by recurrent seizures and is associated with the non-pro-gressive brain disease. In Labradors, the disease occurs most frequently from the ages of six months to three years, and rarely ever over the age of five years. A dog undergoing a seizure usually loses consciousness and experiences stiffness in his limbs. A paddling movement followed by the dog crying, wetting him-self, defecating and/or drooling describes the common occurrence. The dog becomes confused, drowsy and/or disoriented after the seizure. There are certain

> **DID YOU KNOW?**
>
> Purebred enthusiasts have become increasingly aware of congenital and hereditary problems of their dogs. Since breeds like the Labrador Retriever are blest and cursed with such great popularity, many unsound dogs are bred each year. Responsible breeders test their dogs for the many conditions that affect Labrador Retrievers so that pet owners can have a healthy, sound dog that will live into its teens.

drugs available to control the frequency and intensity of the seizures. Since epilepsy is identified as a genetic/hereditary condition in Labrador Retrievers, no animals prone to seizures should be bred. Likewise, the siblings of affected animals should also be excluded from breeding programmes. Spaying affected bitches will reduce seizures as well.

Two other conditions that affect the nervous systems of Labrador Retrievers include narcolespy and cataplexy. Narcolepsy is a sleeping disorder characterised by the animal suddenly falling asleep with no signs of drowsiness, and frequently triggered by vigorous activity. It has been found to be of genetic cause in the Labrador Retriever and affects young pups between one to five months of age. Cataplexy is a similar disorder that involves the sleep-wake cycle being altered. Both conditions are genetically based and therefore no Labradors with either condition should be bred.

Canine hip dysplasia bullies itself to the top of list of most breeds' hereditary problems, and the Labrador is no exception. Although not as badly affected as some other breeds, the incidence of hip dysplasia in Labradors is so high that it is the number-one genetic disease in the breed. Conscientious breeders have reduced the incidence in the breed consid-

erably, to nearly half what it once was. Nevertheless, the incidence still lingers between 12 and 14 percent. Hip dysplasia is basically a malformation of the hip joint. The disease grows worse as the

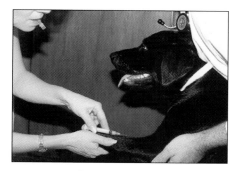

The veterinary surgeon you select should be your Lab's doctor for life.

dog ages, and all dysplastic dogs are born with normal hips. While many dogs are 'susceptible' to hip dysplasia, based on genetic analysis, not all dogs develop the condition. Breeders test that the parents of the litter have been tested for hip dysplasia. This virtually ensures that your puppy will have strong, normal hips. Smart breeders know that hip dysplasia can be 'instigated' by the environment, thus they line their whelping boxes with slip-proof materials (that the puppies can't eat). Studies have proven that puppies who are forced to slip and slide on a hard surface in their whelping boxes have a higher incidence of hip dysplasia. Pet people as well as show people and field people have to be concerned about hip dysplasia. In its severest form, your Labrador will be unable to run and play. Hip dysplasia can grossly compromise the life of your Labrador.

After the age of 16 weeks, your Labrador pup can be tested by a veterinary surgeon. Owners can also lessen the possibility of dysplasia developing by controlling the dog's environment and diet. Breeders recommend feeding a moderate amount of protein and avoiding any foods that are high in calories. Avoid nutritional supplements and feed for a specified interval. Regulate the amount and kind of exercise that your Labrador gets. The breed tends to be somewhat overexuberant in play, so vigorous roughhousing should be avoided for fear of injuring the dog's hips and elbows.

Some Labradors with hip dysplasia experience great discomfort, while others seem only mildly distressed. The ultimate concern of owners is that hip dysplasia contributes to the onset of degenerative joint diseases, such as osteoarthritis, which can render the joint useless.

Predominantly affecting young dogs, elbow dysplasia refers to a system of disorders of the elbow joint. Suffering dogs experience sudden lameness. Arthritis usually develops in the elbow joint. Initial problems

usually manifest themselves when the puppy is four to seven months old. Like hip dysplasia, elbow dysplasia is a congenital defect and no affected animals should be bred. Considering that elbow dysplasia is the less understood and its mode of passing more complicated, it's even more vital that Labradors with elbow dysplasia be excluded from breeding programmes. The disease has been reported in males nearly 50 percent more often than in females. Owners are recommended to follow the same recommendations as for hip dysplasia.

Osteochondrosis (or OCD) affects the cartilage of Labrador Retrievers. The condition is characterised by improperly formed cartilage that forms thick patches on the dog's bones. This excess cartilage is not firmly attached to the dog's bones and causes inflammation. OCD can appear in the stifle joint, shoulder, elbow, or hock. The condition affecting the shoulder is sometimes seen in pups less than six or seven months of age. In Labradors, males are more commonly affected than females. Due to the inability of the affected dog to support his own weight, lameness, usually initially in one leg only, is the first sign.

A common blood disorder, affecting many purebred dogs, is

called von Willebrand's disease. This inherited bleeding disorder, which can be passed by one or both parents, is characterised by a variable lack of blood clotting. It is advisable for all Labrador owners to have their vets perform a test for the level of vWD factor in their dogs' blood. The clotting factor can range from very low (10 to 15%) to very high (60% or more); the higher the factor the more severe the case. Be sure to have your Labrador checked before a spaying or neutering operation. Dogs with less than a 30% clotting factor may have gone undetected until a spaying, and then uncontrollable bleeding occurs or the formation of hematomas. Discuss vWD with your vet to learn more about the disease.

Eye problems have become fairly prevalent in the Labrador Retriever, including progressive retinal atrophy (PRA), cataracts, retinal dysplasia, ectropion, entropion, distichiasis, and others. PRA causes blindness in Labrador Retrievers, affecting the retina and progressively deteriorating it. There is no cure and blindness always results eventually. Breeding animals should be cleared of PRA before being included in a programme.

Cataracts, unlike PRA, rarely cause blindness in the Labrador Retriever. A cataract is visualised as a cloudiness over the lens of the eye. Veterinary science has made it possible to operate to remove a cataract, even though vision is not affected. Animals with cataracts should not be bred since they are hereditary. Likewise, Labradors suffering from retinal dysplasia, causing blindness in young dogs, should not be bred.

Since we have discussed the problem with obesity in

Labs can be afflicted with many physical problems, but vets and breeders have made great strides.

Labradors, we should also discuss the condition known as hypothyroidism. Hypothyroidism, affecting the hormonal system of dogs, is often confused with obesity, though there is no link in reality. Many Labrador owners have concluded that since the only dogs ever detected with hypothyroidism have been greatly overweight that there is a correspondence between the two. Hypothyroidism simply means that the dog is not producing enough thyroid hormones. This disease begins to develop between the ages of one and three, though most owners aren't aware of it until much later. Affected dogs appear lacklustre and without energy; only a

When your Lab defecates you should always clean it up. Also, check that the stool was normal and contained no worms, and that the dog did not strain while moving his bowels.

very small percentage of dogs suffer from obesity. Many dogs lose their fur. Diagnosis is difficult and complicated though the treatment is affordable and very successful. Affected dogs should never be used for breeding.

Some Labradors develop liver disease as young adults. Liver disease in Labradors has been compared to Wilson's disease in humans. A test for copper toxicity can reveal a carrier of this liver disease, which affects a number of breeds and is a major problem in the Bedlington Terrier. The disease is genetically passed and dogs should not be bred.

You can love your dog but you should not engage in mouth-to-mouth contact because your Lab could unwittingly pass worms to you.

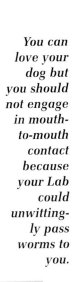

When Your Labrador Retriever Gets Old

The term old is a qualitative term. For dogs, as well as their masters, old is relative. Certainly we can all distinguish between a puppy Labrador Retriever and an adult

Labrador Retriever—there are the obvious physical traits such as size and appearance, and personality traits like their antics and the expressions on their faces. Puppies that are nasty are very rare. Puppies and young dogs like to play with children. Children's natural exuberance is a good match for the seemingly endless energy of young dogs. They like to run, jump, chase and retrieve. When

dogs grow up and cease their interaction with children, they are often thought of as being too old to play with the kids.

On the other hand, if a Labrador Retriever is only exposed to people over 60 years of age, its life will normally be less active and it will not seem to be getting old as soon as its activity level slows down.

If people live to be 100 years old, dogs live to be 20 years old. While this is a good rule of thumb, it is VERY inaccurate. When trying to compare dog years to human years, you cannot make a generalisation about all dogs. You can make the generalisation that, say, 13 years is a

Old Labs look old and act old. Even their personalities can change as they become aged.

DID YOU KNOW?

The bottom line is simply that a dog is getting old when YOU think it is getting old because it slows down in its general activities, including walking, running, eating, jumping and retrieving. On the other hand, certain activities increase, like more sleeping, more licking your hands and body, more barking and more repetition of habits like going to the door when you put your coat on without being called.

good life span for a Labrador Retriever, but you cannot compare it to that of a Chihuahua, as many small breeds typically live longer than large breeds. Dogs are generally considered mature within three years. They can reproduce even earlier. So the first three years of a dog's life are more like seven times that of comparable humans. That means a three-year-old dog is like a 21-year-old person. As the curve of comparison shows, there is no hard and fast rule for comparing dog and human ages. The comparison is made even more difficult, for not all humans age at the same rate...and human females live longer than human males.

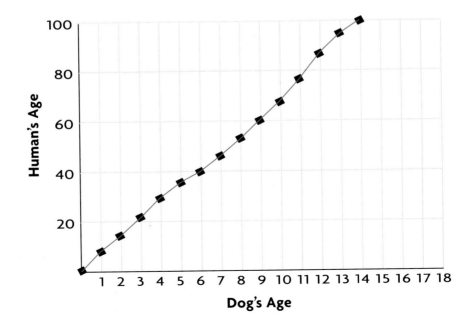

DID YOU KNOW?

The symptoms listed below are symptoms that gradually appear and become more noticeable. They are not life threatening, however, the symptoms below are to be taken very seriously and a discussion with your veterinary surgeon is warranted:

• Your dog cries and whimpers when it moves and stops running completely.

• Convulsions start or become more serious and frequent. The usual convulsion (spasm) is when the dog stiffens and starts to tremble being unable or unwilling to move. The seizure usually lasts for 5 to 30 minutes.

• Your dog drinks more water and urinates more frequently. Wetting and bowel accidents take place indoors without warning.

• Vomiting becomes more frequent.

If the prognosis of the malady indicates the end is near and your beloved pet will only suffer more and experience no enjoyment for the balance of its life, then there is no choice but euthanasia.

WHAT IS EUTHANASIA?

Euthanasia derives from the Greek meaning good death. In other words, it means the planned, painless killing of a dog suffering from a painful, incurable condition, or who is so aged that it cannot walk, see, eat or control its excretory functions.

Euthanasia is usually accomplished by injection with an overdose of an anaesthesia or barbiturate. Aside from the prick of the needle, the experience is painless.

WHAT TO DO WHEN THE TIME COMES

You are never fully prepared to make a rational decision about putting your dog to sleep. It is very obvious that you love your Labrador Retriever or you would not be reading this book. Putting a loved dog to sleep is extremely difficult. It is a decision that must be made with your veterinary surgeon. You are usually forced to make the decision when a life-threatening symptom becomes serious enough for you to seek medical (veterinary) help.

Grey hairs on the muzzle are a sure indication of the dog's becoming old.

HOW ABOUT YOU?

The days during which the dog becomes ill and the end occurs can be unusually stressful for you. If this is your first experience with the death of a loved one, you may need the comfort dictated by your religious beliefs. If you are the head of the family and have children, you should have involved them in the decision of putting your Labrador Retriever to sleep. In any case, euthanasia alone is painful and stressful for the family of the dog. Unfortunately, it does not end there. The decision-making process is just as hard.

Usually your dog can be maintained on drugs for a few days while it is kept in the clinic in order to give you ample time to make a decision. During this time, talking with members of the family or religious representatives, or even people who have lived through this same experience, can ease the burden of your inevitable decision...but then what?

HOW ABOUT THE FINAL RESTING PLACE?

Dogs can have the same privileges as humans. They can be buried in their entirety in a pet cemetery (very expensive) in a burial container, buried in your garden in a place suitably marked with a stone or newly planted tree or bush, cremated with the ashes being given to you, or even stuffed and mounted by a taxidermist.

If you are interested in burying your dog, there are pet cemeteries catering to pet lovers.

All of these options should be discussed frankly and openly with your veterinary surgeon. Do not be afraid to ask financial questions. Cremations are usually mass burning and the ashes you get may not be the ashes of your beloved dog. There are very small crematoriums available to all veterinary clinics. If you want a private cremation, your vet can usually arrange it. However, this may be a little more expensive.

GETTING ANOTHER DOG?

The grief of losing your beloved dog will be as lasting as the grief of losing a human friend or relative. You cannot go out and buy another grandfather, but you can go out and buy another Labrador Retriever. In most cases, if your dog died of old age (if there is such a thing), it had slowed down considerably. Do you want a new Labrador Retriever puppy to replace it? Or are you better off in finding a more mature Labrador Retriever, say two to three years of age, which will usually be housetrained and will have an already developed personality. In this case, you can find out if you like each other after a few hours of being together.

The decision is, of course, your own. Do you want another Labrador Retriever? Perhaps you want a smaller or larger dog? How much do you want to

A resting place for your dog's ashes may be available locally. Contact your veterinary surgeon or local dog club for more information.

spend on a dog? Look in your local newspapers for advertisements (DOGS FOR SALE), or, better yet, consult your local society for the prevention of cruelty to animals to adopt a dog. You may be able to find another Labrador Retriever, or you may choose another breed or a mixed-breed dog. It is harder to find puppies at an animal shelter, but there are often many adult dogs in need of new homes. Private dog kennels specialising in a particular breed are the source for high-quality dogs that they usually breed from champion stock.

Whatever you decide, do it as quickly as possible. Most people usually buy the same breed they had before because they know (and love) the characteristics of that breed. Then, too, they often know people who have the same breed and perhaps they are lucky enough that one of their friends expects a litter soon. What could be better?

CDS: COGNITIVE DYSFUNCTION SYNDROME
"Old Dog Syndrome"

There are many ways to evaluate old-dog syndrome. Veterinary surgeons have defined CDS (cognitive dysfunction syndrome) as the gradual deterioration of cognitive abilities. These are indicated by changes in the dog's behaviour. When a dog changes its routine response, and maladies have been eliminated as the cause of these behavioural changes, then CDS is the usual diagnosis.

More than half the dogs over 8 years old suffer some form of CDS. The older the dog, the more chance it has of suffering from CDS. In humans, doctors often dismiss the CDS behavioural changes as part of 'winding down.'

There are four major signs of CDS: frequent toilet accidents inside the home, sleeps much more or much less than normal, acts confused, and fails to respond to social stimuli.

SYMPTOMS OF CDS

FREQUENT TOILET ACCIDENTS
- *Urinates in the house.*
- *Defecates in the house.*
- *Doesn't signal that he wants to go out.*

SLEEP PATTERNS
- *Moves much more slowly.*
- *Sleeps more than normal during the day.*
- *Sleeps less during the night.*
- *Walks around listlessly and without a destination goal.*

CONFUSION
- *Goes outside and just stands there.*
- *Appears confused with a faraway look in his eyes.*
- *Hides more often.*
- *Doesn't recognise friends.*
- *Doesn't come when called.*

FAILS TO RESPOND TO SOCIAL STIMULI
- *Comes to people less frequently, whether called or not.*
- *Doesn't tolerate petting for more than a short time.*
- *Doesn't come to the door when you return home from work.*

First Aid at a Glance

Burns
Place the affected area under cool water; use ice if only a small area is burnt.

Bee/Insect bites
Apply ice to relieve swelling; antihistamine dosed properly.

Animal bites
Clean any bleeding area; apply pressure until bleeding subsides; go to the vet.

Spider bites
Use cold compress and a pressurised pack to inhibit venom's spreading.

Antifreeze poisoning
Immediately induce vomiting by using hydrogen peroxide.

Fish hooks
Removal best handled by vet; hook must be cut in order to remove.

Snake bites
Pack ice around bite; contact vet quickly; identify snake for proper antivenin.

Car accident
Move dog from roadway with blanket; seek veterinary aid.

Shock
Calm the dog, keep him warm; seek immediate veterinary help.

Nosebleed
Apply cold compress to the nose; apply pressure to any visible abrasion.

Bleeding
Apply pressure above the area; treat wound by applying a cotton pack.

Heat stroke
Submerge dog in cold bath; cool down with fresh air and water; go to the vet.

Frostbite/Hypothermia
Warm the dog with a warm bath, electric blankets or hot water bottles.

Abrasions
Clean the wound and clean out thoroughly with fresh water; apply antiseptic.

 Remember: an injured dog may attempt to bite a helping hand from fear and confusion. Always muzzle the dog before trying to offer assistance.

Showing Your Labrador Retriever

Is the puppy you selected growing into a handsome representative of his breed? You are rightly proud of your handsome little tyke, and he has mastered nearly all of the basic obedience commands that you have taught him. How about attending a dog show and seeing how the other half of the dog-loving world lives! Even if you never imagined yourself standing in the centre ring at the Crufts Dog Show, why not dream a little?

Dog shows can be a lot of fun. Even if you do not participate in the competition, you can observe fine dogs and meet fine people.

The first concept that the canine novice learns when watching a dog show is that each breed first competes against members of its own breed. Once the judge has selected the best member of each breed, then that chosen dog will compete with other dogs in its group. Finally the best of each group will compete for Best in Show and Reserve Best in Show.

The second concept that you must understand is that the dogs are not actually competing with one another. The judge compares each dog against the breed standard, which is a written

description of the ideal specimen of the breed. This imaginary dog never walked into a show ring, has never been bred and, to the woe of dog breeders around the globe, does not exist. Breeders attempt to get as close to this ideal as possible, with every litter, but theoretically the 'perfect' dog is so elusive that it is impossible. (And if the 'perfect' dog were born, breeders

> **DID YOU KNOW?**
> The Kennel Club divides its dogs into seven Groups: Gundogs, Utility, Working, Toy, Terrier, Hounds and Pastoral.*
>
> *The Pastoral Group, established in 1999, includes those sheepdog breeds previously categorised in the Working Group.*

and judges would never agree that it was indeed 'perfect.')

If you are interested in exploring dog shows, your best bet is to join your local breed club. These clubs host shows (often matches and open shows for beginners), send out newsletters, offer training days and provide an outlet to meet members who are often friendly and generous with their advice and contacts. To locate the nearest breed club for you, contact The Kennel Club, the ruling body for the British dog world, not just for conformation shows, but for working trials, obedience trials, agility trials and field trials. The Kennel Club furnishes the rules and regulations for all these events plus general dog registration and other basic requirements of dog ownership. Its annual show, held in Birmingham, is the largest bench show in England.

Photo by Carol Ann Johnson.

In 1998 this Labrador Retriever was the breed record holder in England. This photo shows it receiving its record-breaking CC.

Every year no fewer than 20,000 of the U.K.'s best dogs qualify to participate in Crufts, a marvelous show lasting four days.

In shows held under the auspices of The Kennel Club, which includes Great Britain, Australia, South Africa and beyond, there are different kinds of shows. At the most competitive and prestigious of these shows, the Championship Shows, a dog can earn Challenge Certificates, and thereby become a 'champion.' A dog must earn three Challenge Certificates under three different judges to earn the prefix of 'Sh Ch.' or 'Ch.' Note that some breeds must qualify in a field trial in order to gain the title of full champion. Challenge Certificates are awarded to a very small percentage of the dogs competing, and the number of Challenge Certificates awarded in any one

WINNING THE TICKET

Earning a championship at Kennel Club shows is the most difficult in the world. Compared to the United States and Canada where it is relatively not 'challenging,' collecting three green tickets not only requires much time and effort, it can be very expensive! Challenge Certificates, as the tickets are properly known, are the building blocks of champions— good breeding, good handling, good training and good luck!

year is based upon the total number of dogs in each breed entered for competition. There are three types of Championship Shows, a General Show, where all breeds recognised by The Kennel Club can enter; a Group Show, limited to breeds in a single group; and a Breed Show,

> **DID YOU KNOW?**
>
> Just like with anything else, there is a certain etiquette to the show ring that can only be learned through experience. Showing your dog can be quite intimidating to you as a novice when it seems as if everyone else knows what he's doing. You can familiarise yourself with ring procedure beforehand by taking a class to prepare you and your dog for conformation showing or by talking with an experienced handler. When you are in the ring, listen and pay attention to the judge and follow his/her directions. Remember, even the most skilled handlers had to start somewhere. Keep it up and you too will be a pro in no time!

which is limited to only a single breed.

Open Shows are generally less competitive and are frequently used as 'practice shows' for young dogs. These shows, of which there are hundreds each year, can be invitingly social events and are great first show experiences for the novice. If you're just considering watching

a show to wet your paws, an Open Show is a great choice.

While Championship and Open Shows are most important for the beginner to understand, there are other types of shows in which the interested dog owner can participate. Training clubs, for example, sponsor Matches that can be entered on the day of the show for a nominal fee. These introductory level exhibitions are uniquely run: two dogs are pulled from a raffle and 'matched,' the winner of that match goes on to the next round, and eventually only one dog is left undefeated. Match shows are great fun for the dog enthusiast who wants to compete with his dog without spending a great deal of time and money on the sport of conformation showing.

Exemption shows are similar in that they are simply fun classes and usually held in conjunction with small agricultural shows. Primary shows can also be entered on the day of the event and dogs entered must not have won anything towards their titles. Limited shows must be entered well in advance, and there are limitations upon who can enter. Regardless of which type show you choose to begin with, you and your dog will have a grand time competing and learning your way about the shows.

judge will have the exhibitor move the dog around the ring in some pattern that he or she should specify (another advantage to not going first, but always listen since some judges change their directions, and the judge is always right!) Finally the judge will give the dog one last look before moving on to the next exhibitor.

If you are not in the top three at your first show, do not be discouraged. Be patient and consistent and you will eventually find yourself in the winning lineup. Remember that the winners were once in your shoes

Arriving at the show and trying to find your bench and ring can be a bit exasperating. Have patience!

Before you actually step into the ring, you would be well advised to sit back and observe the judge's ring procedure. If it is your first time in the ring, do not be over-anxious and run to the front of the line. It is much better when you can stand back and study how the exhibitor in front of you is performing. The judge asks each handler to 'stand' the dog, hopefully showing the dog off to his best advantage. The judge will observe the dog from a distance and from different angles, approach the dog, check his teeth, overall structure, alertness and muscle tone, as well as consider how well the dog 'conforms' to the standard. Most importantly, the

Your dog has to respect the judge by standing properly.

Contending dogs are thoroughly examined by the judges and the dogs must readily tolerate such examinations.

and have devoted many hours and much money to earn the placement. If you find that your dog is losing every time and never getting a nod, it may be time to consider a different dog sport or just to enjoy your Labrador Retriever as a pet.

WORKING TRIALS

Working trials can be entered by any well-trained dog of any breed, not just Gundogs or Working dogs. Many dogs that earn the Kennel Club Good Citizen Dog award choose to participate in a working trial. There are five stakes at both open and championship levels: Companion Dog (CD), Utility Dog (UD), Working Dog (WD), Tracking Dog (TD), and Patrol

Dog (PD). As in conformation shows, dogs compete against a standard and if the dog reaches the qualifying mark, it obtains a certificate. Divided into groups, each exercise must be achieved 70 percent in order to qualify. If the dog achieves 80 percent in the open level, it receives a Certificate of Merit (COM); in the championship level, it receives a Qualifying Certificate. At the CD stake, dogs must participate in four groups, Control, Stay, Agility and Search (Retrieve and Nosework). At the next three levels, UD, WD and TD, there are only three groups: Control, Agility and Nosework.

Agility consists of three jumps: a vertical scale, a six-foot wall of planks; a clear jump, a basic three-foot hurdle with a removable top bar; and a long jump of angled planks stretching nine feet.

To earn the UD, WD and TD, dogs must track approximately

CLASSES AT DOG SHOWS

There can be as many as 18 classes per sex for your breed. Check the show schedule carefully to make sure that you have entered your dog in the appropriate class. Among the classes offered can be: Minor Puppy (ages 6 to 9 months); Puppy (ages 6 to 12 months); Junior (ages 6 to 18 months); Beginners (handler or dog never won first place); as well as the following, each of which is defined in the schedule: Maiden; Novice; Tyro; Debutant; Undergraduate; Graduate; Postgraduate; Minor Limit; Mid Limit; Limit; Open; Veteran; Stud Dog; Brood Bitch; Progeny; Brace; and Team.

one-half mile for articles laid from one-half hour to three hours ago. Tracks consist of turns and legs, and fresh ground is used for each participant.

The fifth stake, PD, involves teaching manwork, which of course is not recommended for every breed.

FIELD TRIALS AND WORKING TESTS

Working tests are frequently used to prepare dogs for field trials, the purpose of which is to heighten the instincts and natural abilities of gundogs. Live game is not used in working tests. Unlike field trials, working tests do not count toward a dog's record at the Kennel Club, though the same judges often oversee working tests. Field trials began in England in 1947, and are only moderately popular among dog folk. While breeders of Working and Gundog breeds concern themselves with the field abilities of their dogs, there is considerably less interest in field trials than dog shows. In order for dogs to become full champions, certain breeds must qualify in the field as well. Upon gaining three CCs in the show ring, the dog is designated a Show Champion (Sh Ch). The title Champion (Ch) requires that the dog gain an award at a field trial, be a 'special qualifier' at a field trial or pass a 'special show dog qualifier' judged by a field trial judge on a shooting day.

AGILITY TRIALS

Agility trials began in the United Kingdom in 1977 and have since spread around the world, especially to the United States, where the sport enjoys strong popularity. The handler directs his dog over an obstacle course that includes jumps (such as those used in the working trials), as well as tyres, the dog walk, weave poles, pipe tunnels, collapsed tunnels, etc. The Kennel Club requires that dogs not be trained for agility until they are 12 months old. This dog sport intends to be great fun for dog and owner and interested owners should join a training club that has obstacles and experienced agility handlers who can introduce you and your dog to the 'ropes' (and tyres, tunnels and so on).

Teaching agility does not intend to teach your Lab to climb onto tables in your home.

141

FÉDÉRATION CYNOLOGIQUE INTERNATIONALE

Established in 1911, the Fédération Cynologique Internationale represents the 'world kennel club,' the international body brings uniformity to the breeding, judging and showing of purebred dogs. Although the FCI originally included only European nations, namely France, Holland, Austria and Belgium, the latter of which remains the headquarters, the organisation today embraces nations on six

> **DID YOU KNOW?**
> You can get information about dog shows from kennel clubs and breed clubs:
>
> Fédération Cynologique Internationale
> 14, rue Leopold II
> B-6530 Thuin, Belgium
>
> The Kennel Club
> 1-5 Clarges St., Piccadilly,
> London W1Y 8AB, UK
> www.the-kennel-club.org.uk
>
> American Kennel Club
> 5580 Centerview Drive
> Raleigh, NC 27606-3390, USA
> www.akc.org
>
> Canadian Kennel Club
> 89 Skyway Ave., Suite 100
> Etobicoke, Ontario
> M9W 6R4 Canada
> www.ckc.ca

> **HOW TO ENTER A DOG SHOW**
> 1. Obtain an entry form and show schedule from the Show Secretary.
> 2. Select the classes that you want to enter and complete the entry form.
> 3. Transfer your dog into your name at The Kennel Club. (Be sure that this matter is handled before entering.)
> 4. Find out how far in advance show entries must be made. Oftentimes it's more than a couple of months.

continents and recognises well over 400 breeds of purebred dog. There are three titles attainable through the FCI: the International Champion, which is the most prestigious; the International Beauty Champion, which is based on aptitude certificates in different countries; and the International Trial Champion, which is based on achievement in obedience trials in different countries. Of course, quarantine laws in England and Australia prohibit most exhibitors from entering FCI shows, though the rest of the European Nation does participate in these impressive canine spectacles, the largest of which is the World Dog Show, hosted in a different country each year. FCI sponsors both national and international shows. The hosting country determines the judging system and breed standards are always based on the breed's country of origin.

Understanding Your Dog's Behaviour

As a Labrador Retriever owner, you have selected your dog so that you and your loved ones can have a companion, a protector, a friend and a four-legged family member. You invest time, money and effort to care for and train the family's new charge. Of course, this chosen canine behaves perfectly! Well, perfectly like a dog.

THINK LIKE A DOG

Dogs do not think like humans, nor do humans think like dogs, though we try. Unfortunately, a dog is incapable of figuring out how humans think, so the responsibility falls on the owner to adopt a proper canine mindset. Dogs cannot rationalise, and dogs exist in the present moment. Many dog owners make the mistake in training of thinking that they can reprimand their dog for something he did a while ago. Basically, you cannot even reprimand a dog for something he did 20 seconds ago! Either catch him in the act or forget it! It is a waste of your and your dog's time—in his mind, you are reprimanding him for whatever he is doing at that moment.

The following behavioural problems represent some which owners most commonly encounter. Every dog is unique and every situation is unique. No author could purport to solve your Labrador Retriever's problem simply by reading a script. Here we outline some basic 'dogspeak' so that owners' chances of solving behavioural problems are increased. Discuss bad habits with your veterinary

Your Lab will eagerly retrieve a dummy that you throw. Is he doing this to please you or to enjoy himself...or both? Can you think like a dog?

surgeon and he/she can recommend a behavioural specialist to consult in appropriate cases. Since behavioural abnormalities are the leading reason owners abandon their pets, we hope that you will make a valiant effort to solve your Labrador Retriever's problem. Patience and understanding are virtues that dwell in every pet-loving household.

AGGRESSION

Aggression can be a very big problem in dogs. While a breed like the Labrador Retriever is most often thought of as a very friendly breed and a great family

> **DID YOU KNOW?**
>
> Behavioural specialists catalogue canine aggression to include not only dominant aggression and aggression over other dogs but also fear-induced, intrasexual, learned, protective (food, property, etc.), parental, pain-induced and predatory aggressions. Medical conditions can also spur aggression in dogs, including hypothyroidism, hydrocephalus, hyperthyroidism, hormonal imbalance, and epilepsy.

Most Labs are very friendly, but when someone approaches their turf they will make their presence known.

pet, there is no breed that is completely without aggression. Aggression, when not controlled, becomes dangerous. An aggressive dog, no matter the size, may lunge at, bite or even attack a person or another dog. Aggressive behaviour is not to be tolerated. It is more than just inappropriate behaviour; it is not safe. It is painful for a family to watch their dog become unpredictable in his behaviour to the point where they are afraid of the dog. And while not all aggressive behaviour is dangerous, it can be frightening: growling, baring teeth, etc. It is important to get to the root of the problem to ascertain why the dog is acting in this manner. Aggression is a display of dominance, and the dog should not have the dominant role in its pack, which is, in this case, your family.

It is important not to challenge an aggressive dog as this

The down command should be emphasised when training a potentially dominant dog.

who has experience with the Labrador Retriever specifically. Together, perhaps you can pinpoint the cause of your dog's aggression and do something about it. An aggressive dog cannot be trusted, and a dog that cannot be trusted is not safe to have as a family pet. If the pet Labrador Retriever becomes untrustworthy, he cannot be kept in the home with the family. The

could provoke an attack. Observe your Labrador Retriever's body language. Does he make direct eye contact and stare? Does he try to make himself as large as possible: ears cocked, chest out, tail erect? Height and size signify authority in a dog pack—being taller or 'above' another dog literally means that he is 'above' in the social status. These body signals tell you that your Labrador Retriever thinks he is in charge, a problem that needs to be dealt with. An aggressive dog is unpredictable in that you never know when he is going to strike and what he is going to do. You cannot understand why a dog that is playful and loving one minute is growling and snapping the next.

The best solution is to consult a behavioural specialist, one

DID YOU KNOW?
Dogs and humans may be the only animals that laugh. Dogs imitate the smile on their owner's face when

they greet each other. The dog only smiles at its human friends. It never smiles at another dog or cat. Usually it rolls up its lips and shows its teeth in a clenched mouth while it rolls over onto its back begging for a soft scratch.

You can often read aggression or friendship on a Lab's face, but it's hard to tell what this chocolate Lab is thinking.

warning, he will lunge at and bite the other dog. A way to correct this is to let your Labrador Retriever approach another dog when walking on lead. Watch very closely and at the very first sign of aggression, correct your Labrador Retriever and pull him away. Scold him for any sign of discomfort, and then praise him when he ignores or tolerates the other dog. Keep this up until either he stops the aggressive behaviour, learns to ignore the other dog or even accepts other dogs. Praise him lavishly for his correct behaviour.

DOMINANT AGGRESSION

A social hierarchy is firmly established in a wild dog pack. The dog wants to dominate those under him and please those above him. Dogs know that there must be a leader. If you are not the obvious choice for emperor, the dog will assume the throne! These conflicting innate desires are what a dog owner is up against when he sets about training a dog. In training a dog to obey commands, the owner is reinforcing that he is the top dog in the 'pack' and that the dog should, and should want to, serve his superior. Thus, the owner is suppressing the dog's urge to dominate by modifying his behaviour and making him obedient.

family must get rid of the dog. In the worst case, the dog must be euthanized.

AGGRESSION TOWARD OTHER DOGS

A dog's aggressive behaviour toward another dog stems from not enough exposure to other dogs at an early age. If other dogs make your Labrador Retriever nervous and agitated, he will lash out as a protective mechanism. A dog who has not received sufficient exposure to other canines tends to believe that he is the only dog on the planet. The animal becomes so dominant that he does not even show signs that he is fearful or threatened. Without growling or any other physical signal as a

An important part of training is taking every opportunity to reinforce that you are the leader. The simple action of making your Labrador Retriever sit to wait for his food instead of allowing him to run up to get it when he wants it says that you control when he eats; he is dependent on you for food. Although it may be difficult, do not give in to your dog's wishes every time he whines at you or looks at you with pleading eyes. It is a constant effort to show the dog that his place in the pack is at the bottom. This is not meant to sound cruel or inhumane. You love your Labrador Retriever and you should treat him with care and affection. You (hopefully) did not get a dog just so you could boss around another creature. Dog training is not about being cruel or feeling important, it is about moulding the dog's behaviour into what is acceptable and teaching him to live by your rules. In theory, it is quite simple: catch him in appropriate behaviour and reward him for it. Add a dog into the equation and it becomes a bit more trying, but as a rule of thumb, positive reinforcement is what works best.

With a dominant dog, punishment and negative reinforcement can have the opposite effect of what you are after. It can make a dog fearful and/or

DID YOU KNOW?

Fear in a grown dog is often the result of improper or incomplete socialisation as a pup, or it can be the result of a traumatic experience he suffered when young. Keep in mind that the term 'traumatic' is relative—something that you would not think twice about can leave a lasting negative impression on a puppy. If the dog experiences a similar experience later in life, he may try to fight back to protect himself. Again, this behaviour is very unpredictable, especially if you do not know what is triggering his fear.

act out aggressively if he feels he is being challenged. Remember, a dominant dog perceives himself at the top of the social heap, and will fight to defend his perceived status. The best way to prevent that is to never give him reason to think that he is in control in the first place. If you are having trouble training your Labrador Retriever and it seems as if he is constantly challenging your authority, seek the help of an obedience trainer or behavioural specialist. A professional will work with both you and your dog to teach you effective techniques to use at home. Beware of trainers who rely on excessively harsh methods; scolding is necessary now and then, but the focus in your training should always be on positive reinforcement.

147

If you can isolate what brings out the fear reaction, you can help the dog get over it. Supervise your Labrador Retriever's interactions with people and other dogs, and praise the dog when it goes well. If he starts to act aggressively in a situation, correct him and remove him from the situation. Do not let people approach the dog and start petting him without your express permission. That way, you can have the dog sit to accept petting, and praise him when he behaves properly. You are focusing on praise and on modifying his behaviour by rewarding him when he acts appropriately. By being gentle and by supervising his interactions, you are showing him that there is no need to be afraid or defensive.

Every dog must chew.

SEXUAL BEHAVIOUR

Dogs exhibit certain sexual behaviours that may have influenced your choice of male or female when you first purchased your Labrador Retriever. Spaying/neutering will eliminate these behaviours, but if you are purchasing a dog that you wish to breed, you should be aware of what you will have to deal with throughout the dog's life.

Female dogs usually have two oestruses per year, each season lasting about three weeks. These are the only times in which a female dog will mate, and she usually will not allow this until the second week of the cycle. If a bitch is not bred during the heat cycle, it is not uncommon for her to experience a false pregnancy, in which her mammary glands swell and she exhibits maternal tendencies toward toys or other objects.

Owners must further recognise that mounting is not merely a sexual expression but also one of dominance. Be consistent and persistent and you will find that you can 'move mounters.'

CHEWING

The national canine pastime is chewing! Every dog loves to sink his 'canines' into a tasty bone, but sometimes that bone is attached to his owner's hand! Dogs need to chew, to massage their gums, to make their new teeth feel better and to exercise their jaws. This is a natural behaviour deeply imbedded in all things canine. Our role as owners is not to stop chewing, but to redirect it to positive, chew-worthy objects. Be an informed owner and purchase proper chew toys for your

Labrador Retriever, like strong nylon bones made for large dogs. Be sure that the devices are safe and durable, since your dog's safety is at risk. Again, the owner is responsible for ensuring a dog-proof environment. The best answer is prevention: that is, put your shoes, handbags and other tasty objects in their proper places (out of the reach

DID YOU KNOW?

Males, whether whole or altered, will mount most anything: a pillow, your leg or, much to your horror, even your neighbour's leg. As with other types of inappropriate behaviour, the dog must be corrected while in the act, which for once is not difficult. Often he will not let go! While a puppy, experimenting with his very first urges, his owners feel he needs to 'sow his oats' and allow the pup to mount. As the pup grows into a full-size dog, with full-size urges, it becomes a nuisance and an embarrassment. Males always appear as if they are trying to 'save the race,' more determined and strong than imaginable. While altering the dog at an appropriate age will limit the dog's desire, it usually does not remove it entirely.

of the growing canine mouth). Direct puppies to their toys whenever you see them tasting the furniture legs or the leg of your trousers. Make a loud noise to attract the pup's attention and immediately escort him to his chew toy and engage him with the toy for at least four minutes, praising and encouraging him all the while.

Some trainers recommend deterrents, such as hot pepper or another bitter spice or a product designed for this purpose, to discourage the dog from chewing on unwanted objects. This is sometimes reliable, though not as often as the manufacturers of such products claim. Test out the product with your own dog before investing in a case of it.

You must give your Lab puppy safe, strong chew devices.

JUMPING UP

Jumping up is a dog's friendly way of saying hello! Some dog owners do not mind when their dog jumps up, which is fine for them. The problem arises when guests come to the house and the dog greets them in the same manner—whether they like it or not! However friendly the greet-

149

ing may be, chances are your visitors will not appreciate nearly being knocked over by 35 kgs of Labrador Retriever. The dog will not be able to distinguish upon whom he can jump and whom he cannot. Therefore, it is probably best to discourage this behaviour entirely.

Pick a command such as 'Off' (avoid using 'Down' since you will use that for the dog to lie down) and tell him 'Off' when he jumps up. Place him on the ground on all fours and have him sit, praising him the whole time. Always lavish him with praise and petting when he is in the 'sit' position. That way you are still giving him a warm affectionate greeting, because you are as excited to see him as he is to see you!

A Lab's way of saying hello is often by jumping up to greet you.

DIGGING

Digging, which is seen as a destructive behaviour to humans, is actually quite a natural behaviour in dogs. Even though your Lab is not one of the 'earth dogs' (also known as terriers), his desire to dig can be irrepressible and most frustrating to his owners. When digging occurs in your garden, it is actually a normal behaviour redirected into something the dog can do in his everyday life. For example, in the wild a dog would be actively seeking food, making his own shelter, etc. He would be using his paws in a purposeful manner; he would be using them for his survival. Since you provide him with food and shelter, he has no need to use his paws for these purposes, and so the energy that he would be using manifests itself in the form of little holes all over your garden and flower beds.

Perhaps your dog is digging as a reaction to boredom—it is somewhat similar to someone eating a whole bag of crisps in front of the television—because they are there and there is not anything better to do! Basically, the answer is to provide the dog with adequate play and exercise so that his mind and paws are occupied, and so that he feels as if he is doing something useful.

Of course, digging is easiest to control if it is stopped as soon as possible, but it is often hard to catch a dog in the act, especially if he is alone in the garden during the day. If your dog is a compulsive digger and is not easily distracted by other activities, you can designate an area on your property where it is okay for him to dig. If you catch him digging in an off-limits area of the garden, immediately bring him to the approved area and praise him for digging there. Keep a close eye on him so that you can catch him; that is the only way he is going to understand what is permitted and what is not. If you bring him to a hole he dug an hour ago and tell him 'No,' he will understand that you are not fond of holes, or dirt, or flowers. If you catch him while he is stifle-deep in your tulips, that is when he will get your message.

BARKING

Dogs cannot talk—oh, what they would say if they could! Instead, barking is a dog's way of 'talking.' It can be somewhat frustrating because it is not always easy to tell what a dog means by his bark—is he excited, happy, frightened, angry? Whatever it is that the dog is trying to say, he should not be punished for barking. It is only when the barking becomes excessive, and when the excessive barking becomes a bad habit, does the behaviour need to be modified. If an intruder came into your home in the middle of the night and the dog barked a warning, wouldn't you be pleased? You would probably deem your dog a hero, a wonderful

DID YOU KNOW?

To encourage proper barking, you can teach your dog the command 'quiet.' When someone comes to the door and the dog barks a few times, praise him. Talk to him soothingly and when he stops barking, tell him 'quiet' and continue to praise him. In this sense you are letting him bark his warning, which is an instinctive behaviour, and then rewarding him for being quiet after a few barks. You may initially reward him with a treat after he has been quiet for a few minutes.

guardian and protector of the home. On the other hand, if a friend drops by unexpectedly and rings the doorbell and is greeted with a sudden sharp bark, you would probably be annoyed at the dog. But isn't it just the same behaviour? The dog does not know any better...unless he sees who is at the door and it is someone he is familiar with, he will bark as a means of vocalising that his (and your) territory is being threatened. While your friend is not posing a threat, it is all the same to the dog. Barking is his means of letting you know that there is an intrusion, whether friend or foe, on your property. This type of barking is instinctive and should not be discouraged.

Excessive habitual barking, however, is a problem that should be corrected early on. As your Labrador Retriever grows up, you will be able to tell when his barking is purposeful and when it is for no reason. You will become able to distinguish your dog's different barks and with what they are associated. For example, the bark when someone comes to the door will be different from the bark when he is excited to see you. It is similar to a person's tone of voice, except that the dog has to rely totally on tone of voice because he does not have the benefit of using words. An incessant barker will be evident at an early age.

There are some things that encourage a dog to bark. For example, if your dog barks non-stop for a few minutes and you give him a treat to quieten him, he believes that you are rewarding him for barking. He will associate barking with getting a treat, and will keep doing it until he is rewarded.

FOOD STEALING

Is your dog devising ways of stealing food from your counter tops? If so, you must answer the following questions: Is your Labrador Retriever hungry, or is he 'constantly famished' like every other chow hound? Why is there food on the counter top? Face it, some dogs are more food-motivated than others; some dogs are totally obsessed by a slab of brisket and can only think of their next meal. Food stealing is terrific fun and always yields a great reward— FOOD, glorious food.

The owner's goal, therefore, is to make the 'reward' less rewarding, even startling! Plant a shaker can (an empty pop can with coins inside) on the counter so that it catches your pooch offguard. There are other devices available that will surprise the dog when he is looking for a mid-afternoon snack. Such remote-control devices, though not the first choice of some trainers, allow the correction to come from the object instead of the owner. These devices are also useful to keep the snacking hound from napping on furniture that is forbidden.

BEGGING

Just like food stealing, begging is a favourite pastime of hungry puppies! With that same reward—FOOD! Dogs quickly learn that their owners keep the 'good food' for themselves, and that we humans do not dine on kibble alone. Begging is a conditioned response related to a specific stimulus, time and place. The sounds of the kitchen, cans and bottles opening, crinkling bags, the smell of food in preparation, etc., will excite the chow hound and soon the paws are in the air!

Here is the solution to stopping this behaviour: Never give into a beggar! You are rewarding the dog for sitting pretty, jumping up, whining and rubbing his nose into you by giving him that glorious reward—food. By ignoring the dog, you will (eventually) force the behaviour into extinction. Note that the behaviour likely gets worse before it disappears, so be sure there are not any 'softies' in the family who will give in to little 'Oliver' every time he whimpers, 'More, please.'

SEPARATION ANXIETY

Your Labrador Retriever may howl, whine or otherwise vocalise his displeasure at your leaving the house and his being left alone. This is a normal case of separation anxiety, but there are things that can be done to eliminate this problem. Your dog needs to learn that he will be fine on his own for a while and that he will not wither away

if he is not attended to every minute of the day. In fact, constant attention can lead to separation anxiety in the first place. If you are endlessly coddling and cooing over your dog, he will come to expect this from you all of the time and it will be more traumatic for him when you are not there. Obviously, you enjoy spending time with

> **DID YOU KNOW?**
>
> The number of dogs who suffer from separation anxiety is on the rise as more and more pet owners find themselves at work all day. New attention is being paid to this problem, which is especially hard to diagnose since it is only evident when the dog is alone. Research is currently being done to help educate dog owners about separation anxiety and about how they can help minimise this problem in their dogs.

your dog, and he thrives on your love and attention. However, it should not become a dependent relationship where he is heartbroken without you.

One thing you can do to minimise separation anxiety is to make your entrances and exits as low-key as possible. Do not give your dog a long drawn-out goodbye, and do not lavish him with hugs and kisses when you return. This is giving in to

You must accustom your Lab to being left alone. His crate training will have played an important part in this, and will hopefully minimise the occurrence of separation anxiety.

the attention that he craves, and it will only make him miss it more when you are away. Another thing you can try is to give your dog a treat when you leave; this will not only keep him occupied and keep his mind off the fact that you just left, but it will also help him associate your leaving with a pleasant experience.

You may have to accustom your dog to being left alone in intervals, much like when you introduced your pup to his crate. Of course, when your dog starts whimpering as you approach the door, your first instinct will be to run to him and comfort him, but do not do it! Really—eventually he will adjust and be just fine if you take it in small steps. His anxiety stems from being placed in an unfamiliar situation; by familiarising him with being alone he will learn that he is okay. That is not to say you should purposely leave your dog home alone, but the dog needs to know that while he can depend on you for his care, you do not have to be by his side 24 hours a day.

When the dog is alone in the house, he should be confined to his crate or a designated dog-proof area of the house. This should be the area in which he sleeps, so he should already feel comfortable there and this should make him feel more at ease when he is alone. This is just one of the

many examples in which a crate is an invaluable tool for you and your dog, and another reinforcement of why your dog should view his crate as a 'happy' place, a place of his own.

COPROPHAGIA
Faeces eating is, to most humans, one of the most disgusting behaviours that their dog could engage in, yet to the dog it is perfectly normal. It is hard for us to understand why a dog would want to eat its own faeces: he could be seeking certain nutrients that are missing from his diet, he could be just plain hungry, or he could be attracted by the pleasing (to a dog) scent. While coprophagia most often refers to the dog eating his own faeces, a dog may likely eat that of another animal as well if he comes across it. Vets

have found that diets with a low digestibility, containing relatively low levels of fibre and high levels of starch, increase coprophagia. Therefore, high-fibre diets may decrease the likelihood of dogs eating faeces. Both the consistency of the stool (how firm it feels in the dog's mouth) and the presence of undigested nutrients increase the likelihood. Dogs often find the stool of cats and horses more palatable than that of other dogs. Once the dog develops diarrhoea from faeces eating, it will likely quit this distasteful habit, since dogs tend to prefer eating harder faeces.

To discourage this behaviour, first make sure that the food you are feeding your dog is nutritionally complete and that he is getting enough food. If changes in his diet do not seem to work, and no medical cause can be found, you will have to modify the behaviour through environmental control before it becomes a habit. There are some tricks you can try, such as adding an unpleasant-tasting substance to the faeces to make them unpalatable or adding something to the dog's food which will make it unpleasant tasting after it passes through the dog. The best way to prevent your dog from eating his stool is to make it unavailable—clean up after he eliminates and remove any stool from the garden. If it is not there, he cannot eat it.

DID YOU KNOW?
When a dog bites there is always a good reason for it doing so. Many dogs are trained to protect a person, an area or an object. When that person, area or object is violated the dog will attack. A dog attacks with its mouth. It has no other means of attack. It never uses teeth for defense. It merely runs away or lies down on the ground when it is in an indefensible situation. Fighting dogs (and there are many breeds which fight) are taught to fight, but they also have a natural instinct to fight. This instinct is normally reserved for other dogs, though unfortunate accidents occur when babies crawl towards a fighting dog and the dog mistakes the crawling child as a potential attacker.

If a dog is a biter for no reason, if it bites the hand that feeds it, if it snaps at members of your family, see your veterinarian immediately for behavioural modification treatments.

Never reprimand the dog for stool eating, as this rarely impresses the dog. Vets recommend distracting the dog while he is in the act of stool eating. Another option is to muzzle the dog when he is in the garden to relieve himself; this usually is effective within 30 to 60 days. Coprophagia most frequently is seen in pups 6 to 12 months of age, and usually disappears around the dog's first birthday.

INDEX
Page numbers in boldface indicate illustrations.

My Labrador Retriever

PUT YOUR PUPPY'S FIRST PICTURE HERE

Dog's Name _____

Date _____ Photographer _____